ENVIRONMENT

THIRD EDITION

Ferguson
An imprint of ☑®Facts On File

Careers in Focus: Environment, Third Edition

Copyright © 2004 by Facts On File, Inc.

Ferguson
An imprint of Facts On File, Inc.
132 West 31st Street
New York NY 10001

Careers in focus. Environment. — 3rd ed.
   p. cm.
Includes bibliographical references and index.
   ISBN 0-8160-5550-5 (hc: alk. paper)
   1. Environmental sciences—Vocational guidance—United States—Handbooks, manuals, etc. 2. Environmentalists—Vocational guidance—United States—Handbooks, manuals, etc. 3. Environmental engineering—Vocational guidance—United States—Handbooks, manuals, etc. 4. Environmental engineers—Vocational guidance—United States—Handbooks, manuals, etc. I. Title: Environment. II. J.G. Ferguson Publishing Company.
  GE60.C39 2003
  363.7'0023'73—dc22   2003019347

Ferguson books are available at special discounts when purchased in bulk quantities for businesses, associations, institutions, or sales promotions. Please call our Special Sales Department in New York at (212) 967-8800 or (800) 322-8755.

You can find Ferguson on the World Wide Web at http://www.fergpubco.com

Text design by David Strelecky

Printed in the United States of America

MP FOF 10 9 8 7 6 5 4 3 2 1

This book is printed on acid-free paper.

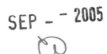

Table of Contents

Introduction

The Environmental Careers Organization (ECO) divides environmental careers into these broad categories: parks and outdoor recreation, air and water quality management, education and communication, hazardous waste management, land and water conservation, fishery and wildlife management, forestry planning, and solid waste management. According to ECO, new kinds of jobs are created all the time to meet new demands. There currently are more than 30 major environment-related areas of study at the college level, and some experts say that the environmental jobs of today are only a small sampling of the types of positions that will constitute this field in the future.

Because of growing concern in the United States and around the world for the future health and survival of the planet, most indicators point to a large growth in the field of environmental sciences. Exactly how large is difficult to project because the level of environmental awareness in this country varies with each political administration and other issues, such as the health of the economy and the tension between creating new jobs and protecting the environment. Media attention devoted to environmental causes—such as preserving the wetlands, saving the rain forests, saving the whales, or recycling—waxes and wanes. Even so, the media help to remind people that significant environmental problems urgently need solutions.

The waning of the nuclear arms race will also promote the growth of environmental careers. Industrialized nations now have more resources to find alternatives to fossil fuels, protect the ozone layer, put a stop to habitat and species destruction, and develop methods for conserving water, energy, and other resources.

Each article in this book discusses a particular environmental occupation in detail. The information primarily comes from Ferguson's *Encyclopedia of Careers and Vocational Guidance*, but each article has been revised and updated with the latest information available. In addition, this edition includes the following new career articles: Environmental Technicians, Fish and Game Wardens, and Naturalists. It also includes illustrative photos of some of the careers, informative sidebars, and interviews with professionals working in the environmental field.

The **Quick Facts** section provides a brief summary of the career, including recommended school subjects, personal skills, work environment, minimum educational requirements, salary ranges, certification or licensing requirements, and employment outlook. This section also provides acronyms and identification numbers for the following government classification indexes: the *Dictionary of Occupational Titles* (DOT), the Guide for Occupational Exploration (GOE), the National Occupational Classification (NOC) Index, and the Occupational Information Network (O*NET)-Standard Occupational Classification System (SOC) index. The DOT, GOE, and O*NET-SOC indexes have been created by the U.S. government; the NOC index is Canada's career classification system. Readers can use the identification numbers listed in the Quick Facts section to access further information on a career. Print editions of the DOT (*Dictionary of Occupational Titles.* Indianapolis, Ind.: JIST Works, 1991) and GOE (*The Complete Guide for Occupational Exploration.* Indianapolis, Ind.: JIST Works, 1993) are available at libraries, and electronic versions of the NOC (http://www23.hrdc-drhc.gc.ca/2001/e/generic/welcome.shtml) and O*NET-SOC (http://online.onetcenter.org) are available on the World Wide Web. When no DOT, GOE, NOC, or O*NET-SOC numbers are present, this means that the U.S. Department of Labor or the Human Resources Development Canada have not created a numerical designation for this career. In this instance, you will see the acronym "N/A," or not available.

The **Overview** section is a brief introductory description of the duties and responsibilities involved in this career. Oftentimes, a career may have a variety of job titles. When this is the case, alternative career titles are presented.

The **History** section describes the history of the particular job as it relates to the overall development of its industry or field.

The **Job** describes the primary and secondary duties of the job.

Requirements discusses high school and postsecondary education and training requirements, any certification or licensing necessary, and any other personal requirements for success in the job.

Exploring offers suggestions on how to gain some experience in or knowledge of the particular job before making a firm educational and financial commitment. The focus is on what can be done while still in high school (or in the early years of college) to gain a better understanding of the job.

The **Employers** section gives an overview of typical places of employment for the job.

Starting Out discusses the best ways to land that first job, be it through the college placement office, newspaper ads, or personal contact.

The **Advancement** section describes what kind of career path to expect from the job and how to get there.

Earnings lists salary ranges and describes the typical fringe benefits.

The **Work Environment** section describes the typical surroundings and conditions of employment—whether indoors or outdoors, noisy or quiet, social or independent, and so on. Also discussed are typical hours worked, any seasonal fluctuations, and the stresses and strains of the job.

The **Outlook** section summarizes the job in terms of the general economy and industry projections. For the most part, Outlook information is obtained from the Bureau of Labor Statistics and is supplemented by information taken from professional associations. Job growth terms follow those used in the *Occupational Outlook Handbook:* Growth described as "much faster than the average" means an increase of 36 percent or more. Growth described as "faster than the average" means an increase of 21 to 35 percent. Growth described as "about as fast as the average" means an increase of 10 to 20 percent. Growth described as "little change or more slowly than the average" means an increase of 0 to 9 percent. "Decline" means a decrease of 1 percent or more.

Each article ends with **For More Information,** which lists organizations that can provide career information on training, education, internships, scholarships, and job placement.

Air Quality Engineers

QUICK FACTS

School Subjects
Biology
Chemistry
Mathematics

Personal Skills
Communication/ideas
Technical/scientific

Work Environment
Primarily indoors
Primarily one location

Minimum Education Level
Bachelor's degree

Salary Range
$23,000 to $35,000 to
$70,000+

Certification or Licensing
Voluntary

Outlook
Faster than the average

DOT
019

GOE
05.01.02

NOC
N/A

O*NET-SOC
N/A

OVERVIEW

Air quality engineers, or *air pollution control engineers,* are responsible for developing techniques to analyze and control air pollution by using sophisticated monitoring, chemical analysis, computer modeling, and statistical analysis. Some air quality engineers are involved in pollution-control equipment design or modification. Government-employed air quality experts keep track of a region's polluters, enforce federal regulations, and impose fines or take other action against those who do not comply with regulations. Privately employed engineers may monitor companies' emissions for certain targeted pollutants to ensure that they are within acceptable levels. Air quality engineers who work in research seek ways to combat or avoid air pollution.

HISTORY

The growth of cities during the industrial revolution was a major contributor to the decline of air quality. Some contaminates (pollutants) have always been with us, such as particulate matter (tiny solid particles) from very large fires and dust caused by wind or mass animal migration. But human populations were not really concentrated enough, nor did the technology exist to produce what is today considered hazardous to the atmosphere, until about 200 years ago. The industrialization of England in the 1750s, followed by France in the 1830s and Germany in the 1850s, changed all that. It created high-density populations as thousands of people were drawn to cities to work in the smoke-belching factories and led to huge increases in airborne pollutants. Work conditions in the factories were notoriously bad, with no pollution-control or safety measures.

Living conditions in cities became very bad: The air became severely polluted and caused respiratory and other diseases.

America's cities were slightly smaller and slower to industrialize, in addition to being more spread out than Old World capitals like London. Even so, levels of sulfur dioxide were so high in Pittsburgh in the early 1900s that ladies' stockings would disintegrate upon prolonged exposure to the air. The rapid growth of the American automobile industry in the first half of the 20th century contributed greatly to air pollution in two ways: initially, from the steel factories and production plants that made economic giants out of places like Pittsburgh and Detroit, and then from the cars themselves. This became an even greater problem as cars enabled people to move out from the fetid industrial city and commute to work there. The increase of private transportation greatly increased auto exhaust and created such modern nightmares as rush hour traffic.

The effects of air pollution were and are numerous. Particulate matter reacts chemically with heat to form ground-level ozone, or smog. Sulfur and nitrogen oxides cause extensive property damage over long periods with their corrosive qualities. Carbon monoxide, the main automobile pollutant, is deadly at a relatively low level of exposure.

Air pollution affects the environment in the form of acid rain and holes in the ozone layer, and in lesser known ways as well. For example, a scientist in Great Britain at the turn of the 20th century followed the evolution of white tree moths as natural selection turned them gray to match the birch trees they used for camouflage, which had become covered with a layer of airborne industrial pollutants. Because pollution is so difficult to remove from the air, and because its effects (loss of atmospheric ozone, for example) are so difficult to alter, the problem tends to be cumulative and an increasingly critical public health issue.

Some private air pollution control was implemented in the 20th century, mainly to prevent factories from ruining their own works with corrosive (strongly acid or caustic) and unhealthy emissions. The first attempt at governmental regulation was the Clean Air Act (1955), but because environmental concerns were not considered viable economic or political issues, this act was not very effective. As environmentalists became increasingly visible and vigorous campaigners, the Air Quality Act was established in 1967. The Environmental Protection Agency (EPA) created National Ambient Air Quality Standards (NAAQS) in 1971, which set limits on ozone, carbon monoxide, sulfur dioxide, lead, nitrogen dioxide, and particulate levels in the emissions of certain industries and processes. States were supposed to design and implement plans to meet the NAAQS, but so few complied that Congress was forced to extend deadlines

Indoor Air Pollution

Although the mention of air pollution might make you think of industrial smokestacks and automotive exhaust, indoor air pollution can also be a very serious problem. How well is your home equipped for pollution control? Your housekeeping habits have much to do with the air quality in your home. The following tips from the Environmental Protection Agency can help you decrease the risks of indoor air pollution:

- Keep your home, including water heater and pipes, well insulated.

- Make sure that all fireplaces and wood-burning stoves are cleaned regularly.

- Paint with a brush, not a sprayer.

- Have a professional check your air conditioning systems in the spring and heating systems in the fall.

- Turn off all appliances when they are not in use.

- Be sure to recycle and remove garbage from your home regularly.

three times. Even now, many goals set by the first generation of air-quality regulations remain unmet, and new pollution issues demand attention. Airborne toxins, indoor air pollution, acid rain, carbon dioxide buildup (the greenhouse effect), and depletion of the ozone are now subjects of international controversy and concern.

THE JOB

The EPA has composed a list of more than 50 regions of the United States that are not in compliance with federal air quality regulations—some dramatically so—and provided deadlines within the next 20 years to bring these areas under control. The EPA regulations cover everything from car emissions to the greenhouse effect and have the weight of law behind them. There are few industries that will not be touched somehow by this legislation and few that will not require the services of an air quality engineer in the years to come.

Air quality engineers are the professionals who monitor targeted industries or sources to determine whether they are operating within acceptable emissions levels. These engineers suggest changes in the setup of specific companies, or even whole industries, to lessen their impact on the atmosphere. There will be ample opportunity in this field to combine interests, precisely because it is a new field with still emerging career paths. An air quality engineer with some background in meteorology, for example, might track the spread of airborne pollutants through various weather systems using computer modeling techniques. Another air quality engineer might research indoor air pollution, discovering causes for the "sick building syndrome" and creating new architectural standards and building codes for safe ventilation and construction materials.

Air quality engineers work for the government, in private industry, as consultants, and in research and development. Government employees are responsible for monitoring a region, citing infractions, and otherwise enforcing government regulations. These workers may be called to give testimony in cases against noncompliant companies. They must deal with public concerns and opinions and are themselves regulated by government bureaucracy and regulations.

Air quality engineers in private industry work within industry or a large company to ensure that air quality regulations are being met. They might be responsible for developing instrumentation to continuously monitor emissions, for example, and using the data to formulate methods of control. They may interact with federal regulators or work independently. Engineers working in private industry also might be involved in what is known as "impact assessment with the goal of sustainable development." This means figuring out the most environmentally sound way to produce products—from raw material to disposal stages—while maintaining or, if possible, increasing the company's profits.

Engineers who work alone as consultants or for consulting firms do many of the same things as engineers in private industry, perhaps for smaller companies who do not need a full-time engineer but still need help meeting federal requirements. They, too, might suggest changes to be implemented by a company to reduce air pollution. Some consultants specialize in certain areas of pollution control. Many private consultants are responsible for selling, installing, and running a particular control system. The job requires some salesmanship and the motivation to maintain a variable clientele.

Finally, engineers committed to research and development may work in public or private research institutions and in academic environments. They may tackle significant problems that affect any number of industries and may improve air quality standards with the discovery of new contaminates that need regulation.

REQUIREMENTS

High School
High school students should develop their skills in chemistry, math, biology, and ecology to prepare for work in air quality engineering.

Since this type of work also involves an understanding of how businesses work and of government regulations, take some general business and government electives, as well.

Postsecondary Training

To break into this field, a bachelor's degree in civil, environmental, or chemical engineering is required. Advancement, specialization, or jobs in research may require a master's degree or Ph.D. Besides the regular environmental or chemical engineering curricula at the college level, future air quality engineers might engage in some mechanical or civil engineering if they are interested in product development. Modelers and planners should have a good knowledge of computer systems. Supporting course work in biology, toxicology, or meteorology can give the job seeker an edge for certain specialized positions even before gaining experience in the workforce.

Certification or Licensing

All engineers who do work that affects public health, safety, or property must register with the state. To obtain registration, engineers must have a degree from an accredited engineering program. Right before they get their degree (or soon after), they must pass an engineer-in-training (EIT) exam covering fundamentals of science and engineering. A few years into their careers, engineers also must pass an exam covering engineering practice.

Other Requirements

Prospective air quality engineers should be puzzle solvers. The ability to work with intangibles is a trait of successful air quality management. As in most fields, communications skills are vital. Engineers must be able to communicate clearly their ideas and findings, both orally and in writing, to a variety of people with different levels of technical understanding.

EXPLORING

Investigating air quality engineering can begin with reading environmental science and engineering periodicals, available in many large libraries. Familiarizing yourself with the current issues involving air pollution will give you a better idea of what problems will be facing this field in the near future.

The next step might be a call to a local branch of the EPA. In addition to providing information about local source problems, they can also provide a breakdown of air quality standards that must be met and who has to meet them.

To get a better idea about college-level course work and possible career directions, contact major universities, environmental associations, or even private environmental firms. Some private consulting firms will explain how specific areas of study combine to create their particular area of expertise.

EMPLOYERS

Most air quality engineers are privately employed in industries subject to emissions control, such as manufacturing. They may also work for the federal government, investigating and ensuring compliance with air quality regulations, as consultants to industry and large companies, and in research and development.

STARTING OUT

Summer positions as an air pollution technician provide valuable insight into the engineer's job as well as contacts and experience. Check with local and state EPA offices and larger consulting firms in your area for internship positions and their requirements. Environmentally oriented engineers may be able to volunteer for citizen watchdog group monitoring programs, patrolling regions for previously undiscovered or unregulated contaminates. Most air quality engineers can expect to get jobs in their field immediately after graduating with a bachelor's degree. Your school placement office can assist you in fine tuning your resume and setting up interviews with potential employers. Government positions are a common point of entry; high turnover rates open positions as experienced engineers leave for the more lucrative private sector, which accounts for four out of five jobs in air quality management. An entry-level job might focus on monitoring and analysis.

ADVANCEMENT

With experience and education, the engineer might develop a specialization within the field of air quality. Research grants are sometimes available to experienced engineers who wish to concentrate on specific problems or areas of study. Management is another avenue of advancement. The demand for technically oriented middle management in the private sector makes engineers with good interpersonal skills very valuable.

In many ways, advancement will be dictated by the increasing value of air quality engineers to business and industry in general. Successful development of air pollution control equipment or systems—perhaps that even cut costs as they reduce pollution—will make air quality engineers important players in companies' economic strategies. As regulations tighten and increasing emphasis is put on minimizing environmental impact, air quality engineers will be in the spotlight as both regulators and innovators. Advancement may come in the form of monetary incentives, bonuses, or management positions over other parts of the organization or company.

EARNINGS

Salaries for entry-level engineers start at around $23,000 to $35,000 per year. Local government agencies pay at the lower end of the scale, state and federal agencies pay slightly more. Salaries in the private sector are highest, from $30,000 up to $70,000 or more. Other benefits may include tuition reimbursement programs, use of a company vehicle for fieldwork, full health coverage, and retirement plans.

WORK ENVIRONMENT

Working conditions differ depending on the employer, the specialization of the position, and the location of the job. An air quality engineer may be required to perform fieldwork, such as observing emission sources, but more often works in an office, determining the factors responsible for airborne pollutants and devising ways to prevent them. Coworkers may include other environmental engineers, lab technicians, and office personnel. An engineer may discuss specific problems with a company's economic planners and develop programs to make that company more competitive environmentally and economically. Those who monitor emissions have considerable responsibility and therefore considerable pressure to do their job well—failure to maintain industry standards could cost their employer government fines. Engineers in some consulting firms may be required to help sell the system they develop or work with.

Most engineers work a standard 40-hour week, putting in overtime to solve critical problems as quickly as possible. A large part of the job for most air quality engineers consists of keeping up to date with federal regulations, industry and regional standards, and developments in their area of expertise. Some employers require standard business attire, while some require more fieldwork from their engineers and may not enforce rigorous dress codes. Unlike water and soil pollution, air pollution can sometimes be difficult to measure quantitatively if the source is unknown. Major pollutants are generally easily identified (although not so easily eliminated), but traces of small "leaks" may literally change with the wind and make for time-consuming, deliberate, and frustrating work.

OUTLOOK

When the immediate scramble to modify and monitor equipment slackens as government regulations are met in the next 20 years, the focus in air quality engineering will shift from traditional "end of pipe" controls (e.g., modifying catalytic converters or gasoline to make cars burn gas more cleanly) to source control (developing alternative fuels and eliminating oil-based industrial emissions). As mentioned, impact assessment will play a large part on the corporate side of air quality management, as businesses strive to stay profitable in the wake of public health and safety regulations. Air pollution problems like greenhouse gas buildup and ozone pollution will not be disappearing in the near future and will be increasingly vital areas of research. International development will allow American pollution control engineers to offer their services in any part of the world that has growing industries or population. Pollution control in general has a big future: Air pollution control is quickly taking up a major chunk of the expected expenditures and revenues in this category.

FOR MORE INFORMATION

For information on student chapters, scholarships, and a list of colleges and degrees offering environmental degrees, contact
Air and Waste Management Association
420 Fort Duquesne Boulevard
One Gateway Center, Third Floor
Pittsburgh, PA 15222
Tel: 412-232-3444
Email: info@awma.org
http://www.awma.org

The following are government pollution control boards:
**State and Territorial Air Pollution Program Administrators/
    Association of Local Air Pollution Control Officials**
444 North Capitol Street, NW, Suite 307
Washington, DC 20001
Tel: 202-624-7864

Email: 4clnair@sso.org
http://www.cleanairworld.org

For general information about air quality and other environmental issues, contact
U.S. Environmental Protection Agency
Ariel Rios Building
1200 Pennsylvania Avenue, NW
Washington, DC 20460
Tel: 202-260-2090
http://www.epa.gov

Ecologists

OVERVIEW

Ecology is the study of the interconnections between organisms (plants, animals) and the physical environment. It links biology, which includes both zoology (the study of animals) and botany (the study of plants), with physical sciences, such as geology and paleontology. Thus, *ecologist* is a broad name for any of a number of different biological or physical scientists concerned with the study of plants or animals within their environment.

HISTORY

Much of the science that ecologists use is not new. The ancient Greeks recorded their observations of natural history many centuries ago. However, linking together the studies of life and the physical environment is fairly new. The term "ecology" was first defined in 1866 by Ernst von Haeckel, a German biologist. Like many scientists of his time, he grappled with Charles Darwin's theory of evolution based on natural selection. This theory said that those species of plants and animals that were best adapted to their environment would survive. Although Haeckel did not agree with Darwin, he and many other scientists grew fascinated with the links between living things and their physical environment. At that time, very important discoveries in geology proved that many forms of plants and animals had once existed but had died out. Fossils showed startlingly unfamiliar plant types, for example, as well as prehistoric animal remains that no one had ever imagined existed. Before such discoveries, people assumed that the species they saw all around them had always existed. Realization that there were important connections between living things and

QUICK FACTS

School Subjects
Biology
Chemistry

Personal Skills
Communication/ideas
Technical/scientific

Work Environment
Primarily outdoors
Primarily multiple locations

Minimum Education Level
Bachelor's degree

Salary Range
$24,000 to $49,239 to
$91,000+

Certification or Licensing
Voluntary

Outlook
Faster than the average

DOT
040

GOE
02.02.02

NOC
2121

O*NET-SOC
N/A

their physical environment was a key step in the development of the science of ecology.

Like most of the other environmental careers, the professional field of ecology did not really grow popular until the late 1960s and early 1970s. Before then, some scientists and others had tried to warn the public about the ill effects of industrialization, unchecked natural resource consumption, overpopulation, spoiling of wilderness areas, and other thoughtless misuse of the environment. But not until the years after World War II (with growing use of radiation and of pesticides and other chemicals, soaring industrial and automobile pollution, and increasing discharge into waterways) did widespread public alarm about the environment grow. By this time, many feared it was too late. Heavy municipal and industrial discharge into Lake Erie, for example, made the lake unsuitable for sustaining life.

In response, the U.S. government passed a series of hard-hitting environmental laws during the 1960s and 1970s. To become compliant with these laws, companies and municipalities began to look around for professionals who understood the problems and could help take steps to remedy them. Originally, they drew professionals from many existing fields, such as geologists, sanitary engineers, biologists, and chemists. These professionals may not have studied environmental problems as such at school, but they were able to apply the science they knew to the problems at hand.

To some extent, this continues to be true today. Many people working on environmental problems still come from general science or engineering backgrounds. Recently, however, there has been a trend toward specialization. Students in fields such as biology, chemistry, engineering, law, urban planning, and communications can obtain degrees with specialization in the environment. An ecologist today can either have a background in traditional biological or physical sciences or have studied these subjects specifically in the context of environmental problems.

THE JOB

The main unit of study in ecology is the ecosystem. Ecosystems are communities of plants and animals within a given habitat that provide the necessary means of survival, including food and water. Ecosystems are defined by such physical conditions as climate, altitude, latitude, and soil and water characteristics. Examples include forests, tundra, savannas (grasslands), and rainforests.

There are many complex and delicate interrelationships within an ecosystem. For example, green plants use the energy of sunlight to make carbohydrates, fats, and proteins; some animals eat these plants and acquire part of the energy of the carbohydrates, fats, and proteins; other animals eat these animals and acquire a smaller part of that energy. Cycles of photosynthesis, respiration, and nitrogen fixation continuously recycle the chemicals of life needed to support the ecosystem. Anything that disrupts these cycles, such as droughts or air or water pollution, can disrupt the delicate workings of the entire ecosystem.

Therefore, a primary concern of ecologists today is to study and attempt to find solutions for disruptions in various ecosystems. Increasingly, an area of expertise is the reconstruction of ecosystems—that is, the restoration of ecosystems that are destroyed or almost completely destroyed because of pollution, overuse of land, or other activities.

According to the Environmental Careers Organization, a key area of work for ecologists is in land and water conservation. They help to restore damaged land and water as well as to preserve wild areas for the future. Understanding the links between organisms and their physical environments can be invaluable in such efforts. This is also true for environmental planning and resource management. Planning involves studying and reporting the impact of an action on the environment. For example, how might the construction of a new federal highway affect the surrounding ecosystem? A planning team may go to the site to view the physical geography and environment, the plants, and the animals. It also may recommend alternative actions that will have less damaging effects.

Resource management means determining what resources already exist and working to use them wisely. Professionals may build databases cataloging the plants, animals, and physical characteristics of a given area. They also may report on what can be done to ensure that the ecosystem can continue to sustain itself in the future. If an ecosystem has been completely destroyed, ecologists can help reconstruct it, getting the physical environment back up to par and reintroducing the species that used to live there.

Ecologists work in many areas of specialization. *Limnologists* study freshwater ecology, *hydrogeologists* focus on water on or below the surface of the earth, *paleontologists* study the remains of ancient life-forms in the form of fossils, *geomorphologists* study the origin of landforms and their changes, and *geochemists* study the chemistry of the earth, including the effect of pollution on the earth's chemistry. Other specialties are those of the endangered species biologists and wetlands ecologists.

REQUIREMENTS
High School
If you are interested in becoming an ecologist, you should take a college prep curriculum while in high school. Classes that will be of particular benefit include Earth science, biology, chemistry, English, and math. Because computers are so often involved in various aspects of research and documentation, you should also take computer science courses.

Postsecondary Training
A bachelor of science degree is the minimum degree required for nonresearch jobs, which include testing and inspection. A master's degree is necessary for jobs in applied research or management. A Ph.D. generally is required to advance in the field, including into administrative positions.

The Environmental Careers Organization suggests that if you can only take one undergraduate major, it should be in the basic sciences: biology, botany, zoology, chemistry, physics, or geology. At the master's degree level, natural resource management, ecology, botany, conservation biology, and forestry studies are useful.

Certification or Licensing
The Ecological Society of America offers professional certification at three levels: associate ecologist, ecologist, and senior ecologist. A candidate's certification level will depend on the amount of education and professional experience he or she has. The society encourages certification as a way to enhance ecologists' professional standing in society.

Other Requirements
Ecologists should appreciate and respect nature, and they must also be well versed in scientific fundamentals. Ecologists frequently, but not always, are naturally idealistic. They should be able to work with other people on a team and to express their special knowledge to the other people on the team, who may have different areas of specialization.

EXPLORING
You can seek more information about ecology from guidance counselors and professional ecologists who work at nearby colleges, universities, and government agencies. An easy way for you to learn more about ecology is to study your own environment. Trips to a nearby pond, forest, or park over the course of several months will provide

opportunities to observe and collect data. Science teachers and local park service or arboretum personnel can also offer you guidance.

EMPLOYERS

By far, the majority of land and water conservation jobs (about 75 percent) are in the public sector, according to the Environmental Careers Organization. This includes the federal government, the largest employer. The Bureau of Land Management, the U.S. Fish and Wildlife Service, the National Park Service, and the U.S. Geological Survey are among the federal agencies that manage U.S. conservation. Other public sector opportunities are with states, regions, and towns. Opportunities in the private sector can be found with utilities, timber companies, and consulting firms. An additional area of employment is in teaching.

STARTING OUT

Internships provide an excellent point of entry into this field. You can volunteer with such groups as the Student Conservation Association (SCA), which places people in resource management projects. Programs include three- to five-week summer internships for high school students. If you have already graduated from high school (and are over age 18), you can check with SCA for internships in forest, wildlife, resource, and other agencies.

Another option is to contact a federal or local government agency directly about an internship. Many, including the Environmental Protection Agency, National Park Service, and Bureau of Land Management, have internship programs. Programs are more informal at the local level.

As for the private sector, an internship with a nonprofit organization may be possible. Such groups include the National Wildlife Federation and the Natural Resources Defense Council.

Entry-level ecologists also may take advantage of temporary or seasonal jobs to gain experience and establish crucial contacts in the field.

ADVANCEMENT

Mid-level biological scientists may move to managerial positions within biology or to nontechnical administrative, sales, or managerial jobs. Ecologists with Ph.D.'s may conduct independent research, advance into administrative positions, or teach on the college level, advancing from assistant professor to associate and tenured professorships.

EARNINGS

Salaries for ecologists vary depending on such factors as their level of education, experience, area of specialization, and the organization for which they work. For example, job postings for June 2000 on the Ecological Society of America's website listed a visiting instructor position at a college offering an annual salary of $24,000. The website also listed an opening for an experienced research plant physiologist at the United States Forest Service that would pay $59,623 to $91,589, depending on the person's experience. In 2000, the U.S. Department of Labor reported the median annual income of biological scientists, which includes ecologists, was $49,239. Ecologists working for the federal government in 2001 earned average salaries of $61,936.

Federal agency jobs tend to pay more than state or local agency jobs. Private sector jobs tend to pay more than public sector jobs.

WORK ENVIRONMENT

Ecologists can work in a variety of places, from wilderness areas to forests to mountain streams. Ecologists also might work in sewage treatment plants, spend their days in front of computers or in research laboratories, or find themselves testifying in court. A certain amount of idealism probably is useful, though not required. It takes more than just loving nature to be in this field; a person has to be good at scientific fundamentals. Ecologists might start out in the field collecting samples, making notes about animal habits, or doing other monitoring. They may need to be able to work as part of a team and express what they know in terms that everyone on the team can understand.

OUTLOOK

Environmentally oriented jobs are expected to increase at a faster rate than the average for all occupations through 2010, according to the U.S. Department of Labor. Land and resource conservation jobs tend to be the most scarce, however, because of high popularity and tight budgets for such agencies. Those with advanced degrees will fare better than ecologists with only bachelor's degrees.

FOR MORE INFORMATION

For information on careers in the geosciences, contact
American Geological Institute
4220 King Street
Alexandria, VA 22302-1502
Tel: 703-379-2480
http://www.agiweb.org

In addition to certification, ESA offers a wide variety of publications, including Issues in Ecology, *and fact sheets about specific ecological concerns. For more information contact*
Ecological Society of America (ESA)
1707 H Street, NW, Suite 400
Washington, DC 20006
Tel: 202-833-8773
Email: esahq@esa.org
http://esa.org

For information on paid internships and careers in the field, contact
Environmental Careers Organization
179 South Street
Boston, MA 02111
Tel: 617-426-4375
http://www.eco.org

For information on internships, job opportunities, and student chapters, contact
National Wildlife Federation
11100 Wildlife Center Drive
Reston, VA 20190-5362
Tel: 703-438-6000
http://www.nwf.org

For information on student volunteer activities and programs, contact
Student Conservation Association
689 River Road
PO Box 550
Charlestown, NH 03603
Tel: 603-543-1700
Email: ask-us@sca-inc.org
http://www.thesca.org/

Environmental Engineers

QUICK FACTS

School Subjects
Mathematics
Physics

Personal Skills
Leadership/management
Technical/scientific

Work Environment
Indoors and outdoors
Primarily multiple locations

Minimum Education Level
Bachelor's degree

Salary Range
$37,210 to $57,780 to
$87,290+

Certification or Licensing
Recommended

Outlook
Faster than the average

DOT
005

GOE
05.01.07

NOC
2131

O*NET-SOC
17-2081.00

OVERVIEW

Environmental engineers design, build, and maintain systems to control waste streams produced by municipalities or private industry. Such waste streams may be wastewater, solid waste, hazardous waste, or contaminated emissions to the atmosphere (air pollution). Environmental engineers typically are employed by the Environmental Protection Agency (EPA), by private industry, or by engineering consulting firms. There are about 52,000 environmental engineers employed in the United States.

HISTORY

Although people have been doing work that falls into the category of environmental engineering for decades, it is only within about the last 30 years that a separate professional category has been recognized for environmental engineers.

Post-Civil-War industrialization and urbanization created life-threatening water and air quality problems. These problems continued during and after World War II, dramatically increasing all forms of environmental pollution. After the war, pollution control technologies were developed to deal with the damage.

"In the 1930s, 1940s, 1950s, even the 1960s, someone who wanted to be an environmental engineer would have been steered toward sanitary engineering, which basically deals with things like wastewater, putting sewers down," says Lee DeAngelis, regional director of the Environmental Careers Organization (ECO).

Sanitary engineering is a form of civil engineering. "Civil engineering is engineering for municipalities," explains Mike Waxman, who heads the environmental training arm of the outreach department at the University of Wisconsin-Madison College of Engineering. "It includes things like building roads, highways, buildings. But a big part of civil engineering is dealing with the waste streams that come from cities or municipalities. Wastewater from a city's sewage treatment plants is a prime example," Waxman says. This water must be treated in order to be pure enough to be used again. "*Scientists* work out what must be done to break down the harmful substances in the water, such as by adding bacteria; engineers design, build, and maintain the systems needed to carry this out. *Technicians* monitor the systems, take samples, run tests, and otherwise ensure that the system is working as it should."

This structure—scientists deciding what should be done at the molecular or biological level, engineers designing the systems needed to carry out the project, and technicians taking care of the day-to-day monitoring of the systems—is applied to other waste streams as well, Waxman adds.

Environmental engineering is an offshoot of civil engineering/sanitary engineering and focuses on the development of the physical systems needed to control waste streams. Civil engineers who already were doing this type of work began to refer to themselves as environmental engineers around 1970 with the great boom in new environmental regulations, according to Waxman. "It's what they wanted to be called," he says. "They wanted the recognition for what they were doing."

THE JOB

There is a small pond in Crawford County, Illinois, that serves as the habitat and primary food source for several different species of fish, frogs, turtles, insects, and birds, as well as small mammals. About a half-mile away is the Jack J. Ryan and Sons Manufacturing Company. For years, this plant has safely treated its wastewater—produced during the manufacturing process—and discharged it into the pond. Then one day, without warning, hundreds of dead fish wash up on the banks of the pond. What's going on? What should be done? It is the job of environmental engineers to investigate and design a system to make the water safe for the flora and fauna that depend on it for survival.

Environmental engineers who work for the federal or state Environmental Protection Agency (EPA) act as police officers or

An environmental engineer collects lake water to test for pollutants. (Corbis)

detectives. They investigate problems stemming from systems that aren't functioning properly. They have knowledge about waste water treatment systems and have the authority to enforce environmental regulations.

The Crawford County pond is in the jurisdiction of the Champaign regional office of the Illinois Environmental Protection Agency (IEPA). There are three divisions: air, land, and water. An environmental engineer in the water division would be alerted to the fish kill at the pond and head out to the site to investigate. The engineer takes photographs and samples of the water and makes notes to document the problem. He or she considers the possibilities: Is it a discharge problem from Jack J. Ryan and Sons? If so, was there an upset in the process? A spill? A flood? Could a storage tank be leaking? Or is the problem further upstream? The pond is connected to other waterways, so could some other discharger be responsible for killing the fish?

The engineer visits Jack J. Ryan and Sons to talk to the production manager and ask if the plant has been doing anything differently lately. The investigation might include a tour of the plant or an examination of its plans. It might also include questioning other manufacturers further upstream, to see if they are doing something new that's caused the fish kill.

Once the problem has been identified, the environmental engineer and the plant officials can work together on the solution. For example, the production manager at Jack J. Ryan and Sons reports that they've changed something in the manufacturing process to produce a new kind of die-cast part. They didn't know they were doing something wrong. The EPA engineer informs the company they'll be fined $10,000, and a follow-up investigation will be conducted to make sure it has complied with regulations.

Jack J. Ryan and Sons may have its own environmental engineer on staff. This engineer's job is to help keep the company in compliance with federal and state regulations while balancing the economic concerns of the company. At one time, industries' environmental affairs positions were often filled by employees who also had other positions in the plant. Since the late 1980s, however, these positions are held by environmental experts, including scientists, engineers, lawyers, and communications professionals.

In the Crawford County pond scenario, a Ryan and Sons environmental expert might get a call from an engineer at the IEPA: "There seems to be a fish kill at the pond near your plant. We've determined it's probably from a discharge from your plant." The Ryan and Sons expert looks at the plant's plans, talks to the production manager, and figures out a plan of action to bring the company into compliance.

Some companies rely on environmental engineering consulting firms instead of keeping an engineer on staff. Consulting firms usually provide teams that visit the plant, assess the problem, and design a system to get the plant back into compliance. Consulting firms not only know the technical aspects of waste control, but also have expertise in dealing with the government—filling out the required government forms, for example.

Broadly speaking, environmental engineers may focus on one of three areas: air, land, or water. Air includes air pollution control, air quality management, and other specialties involved in systems to treat emissions. The private sector tends to have the majority of these jobs, according to the ECO. Land includes landfill professionals, for whom environmental engineering and public health are key areas. Water includes activities like those described above.

A big area for environmental engineers is hazardous waste management. Expertise in designing systems and processes to reduce, recycle, and treat hazardous waste streams is very much in demand, according to ECO. This area tends to be the most technical of all the environmental fields and so demands more professionals with graduate and technical degrees.

Environmental engineers spend a lot of time on paperwork—including writing reports and memos and filling out forms. They also might climb a smokestack, wade in a creek, or go toe-to-toe with a district attorney in a battle over a compliance matter. If they work on company staffs, they may face frustration over not knowing what is going on in their own plants. If they work for the government, they might struggle with bureaucracy. If they work for a consultant, they may have to juggle the needs of the client (including the need to keep costs down) with the demands of the government.

REQUIREMENTS

High School
A bachelor's degree is mandatory to work in environmental engineering. At the high school level, the most important course work is in science and mathematics. It's also good to develop written communication skills. Competition to get into the top engineering schools is tough, so it's important to do well on your ACT or SAT tests.

Postsecondary Training
About 20 schools offer an undergraduate degree in environmental engineering. Another possibility is to earn a civil engineering, mechanical engineering, industrial engineering, or other traditional engineering degree with an environmental focus. You could also obtain a traditional engineering degree and acquire the environmental knowledge on the job or obtain a master's degree in environmental engineering.

Certification or Licensing
If your work as an engineer affects public health, safety, or property, you must register with the state. To obtain registration, you must have a degree from an accredited engineering program. Right before you get your degree (or soon after), you must pass an engineer-in-training (EIT) exam covering fundamentals of science and engineering. A few years after you've started your career, you also must pass an exam covering engineering practice. Additional certification is voluntary and may be obtained through such organizations as the American Academy of Environmental Engineers.

Other Requirements
Environmental engineers must like solving problems and have a good background in science and math. They must be able to, in the words of one engineer, "just get in there and figure out what needs to be done." Engineers must be able to communicate verbally and in writing with a variety of people from both technical and nontechnical backgrounds.

EXPLORING
A good way to explore becoming an environmental engineer is to talk to someone in the field. Contact your local EPA office, check the Yellow Pages for environmental consulting firms in your area, or ask a local industrial company if you can visit. The latter is not as far-fetched as you might think: big industry has learned the value of earning positive community relations, and their outreach efforts may include having an open house for their neighbors in which one can walk through their plants, ask questions, and get a feel for what goes on there.

You cannot practice being an environmental engineer without having a bachelor's degree. However, you can put yourself in situations in which you're around environmental engineers to see what they do and how they work. To do so, you may volunteer for the local chapter of a nonprofit environmental organization, do an internship through ECO or another organization, or work first as an environmental technician, a job that requires less education (such as a two-year associate's degree or even a high school diploma).

Another good way to get exposure to environmental engineering is to familiarize yourself with professional journals. Two journals that may be available in your library include *Chemical & Engineering News,* which regularly features articles on waste management systems, and *Pollution Engineering,* which features articles of interest to environmental engineers.

EMPLOYERS

Environmental engineers most often work for the Environmental Protection Agency (EPA), in private industry, or at engineering consulting firms.

STARTING OUT

The traditional method of entering this field is by obtaining a bachelor's degree and applying directly to companies or to the EPA. School placement offices can assist you in these efforts.

ADVANCEMENT

After environmental engineers have gained work experience, there are several routes for advancement. Those working for the EPA can become a department supervisor or switch to private industry or consulting. In-house environmental staff members may rise to supervisory positions. Engineers with consulting firms may become project managers or specialists in certain areas.

Environmental careers are evolving at a breakneck speed. New specialties are emerging all the time. Advancement may take the form of getting involved at the beginning stages of a new subspecialty that suits an engineer's particular interests, experience, and expertise.

EARNINGS

According to ECO, average solid waste management pay is slightly lower than that for hazardous waste management. Entry-level salaries for professionals in this field range from less than $20,000 to $30,000, with engineers at the higher end of the scale. In water quality management, the range is about $30,000 to $40,000 for state and federal government jobs and $30,000 and up for private jobs.

The *Occupational Outlook Handbook* reports that median annual earnings of environmental engineers were $57,780 in 2000. Salaries ranged from less than $37,210, to more than $87,290. According to a 2001 salary survey by the National Association of Colleges and Employers, bachelor's degree candidates in environmental engineering received starting offers averaging $51,167 a year.

According to the American Academy of Environmental Engineers, engineers with a bachelor of science degree were receiving starting salaries ranging from $36,000 to $42,000 with some as much as $48,000 in the late 1990s. Those with a master's degree earned $40,000–$45,000, and those with a Ph.D. earned $42,000–$50,000. Licensed engineers with five years of experience can expect to earn from $50,000 to $60,000.

Fringe benefits vary widely depending on the employer. State EPA jobs may include, for example, two weeks of vacation, health insurance, tuition reimbursement, use of company vehicles for work, and similar perks. In-house or consulting positions may add additional benefits to lure top candidates.

WORK ENVIRONMENT

Environmental engineers split their time between working in an office and working out in the field. They may also spend time in courtrooms. Since ongoing education is crucial in most of these positions, engineers must attend training sessions and workshops and study new regulations, techniques, and problems. They usually work as part of a team that may include any of a number of different specialists. Engineers must also give presentations of technical information to those with both technical and nontechnical backgrounds.

OUTLOOK

The 1980s were a time of increased environmental regulation and enforcement. Superfund legislation forced states to clean up hazardous waste sites, and the U.S. Environmental Protection Agency required companies to reduce waste and dispose of it more responsibly. Environmental engineers, consequently, had abundant opportunities. In the 1990s, many of the major cleanup efforts were undertaken or finished, causing the environmental engineering job market to taper off from its rapid growth.

The *Occupational Outlook Handbook* projects that there will be faster than average employment growth for environmental engineers through 2010. They will be needed to clean up existing hazards and help companies comply with government regulations. The shift toward prevention of problems and protecting public health should create job opportunities.

Jobs are available with all three major employers—the EPA, industry, and consulting firms. The EPA has long been a big employer of environmental engineers.

FOR MORE INFORMATION

For information on certification, careers, and salaries or a copy of Environmental Engineering Selection Guide *(giving names of accredited environmental engineering programs and of professors who have board certification as environmental engineers), contact*
American Academy of Environmental Engineers
130 Holiday Court, Suite 100
Annapolis, MD 21401
Tel: 410-266-3311
http://www.enviro-engrs.org

For information on internships and career guidance, contact
Environmental Careers Organization
179 South Street
Boston, MA 02111
Tel: 617-426-4375
http://www.eco.org

For career guidance information or a videotape explaining many types of engineering, contact
Junior Engineering Technical Society, Inc.
1420 King Street, Suite 405
Alexandria, VA 22314-2794
Tel: 703-548-5387
Email: jets@nae.edu
http://www.jets.org

The following is a cross-disciplinary environmental association:
National Association of Environmental Professionals
PO Box 2086
Bowie, MD 20718
Tel: 888-251-9902
http://www.naep.org

For information about the private waste services industry, contact
National Solid Wastes Management Association
4301 Connecticut Avenue, NW, Suite 300
Washington, DC 20008
Tel: 800-424-2869
http://www.nswma.org/

Contact SCA for information about internships for high school students.

Student Conservation Association (SCA)
689 River Road
PO Box 550
Charlestown, NH 03603-0550
Tel: 603-543-1700
http://www.thesea.org

Environmental Lobbyists

QUICK FACTS

School Subjects
English
Government
Speech

Personal Skills
Communication/ideas
Helping/teaching
Leadership/management

Work Environment
Primarily indoors
Primarily multiple locations

Minimum Education Level
Bachelor's degree

Salary Range
$12,000 to $40,000 to $80,000

Certification or Licensing
None available

Outlook
About as fast as the average

DOT
165

GOE
11.09.03

NOC
N/A

O*NET-SOC
N/A

OVERVIEW

Lobbyists are people who strive to influence legislation on behalf of a special interest group or a client. Like other lobbyists, *environmental lobbyists* strive to influence state or federal legislation in order to achieve a goal or to benefit a special interest group. Environmental lobbyists, however, deal specifically with environmental issues. They urge legislators and other government officials to support measures that will protect endangered species, limit the exploitation of natural resources, and impose stricter anti-pollution regulations.

HISTORY

Occasionally looked upon as mere influence peddlers, lobbyists actually serve an important role in the democratic process. Government officials and legislators must understand and make decisions about innumerable issues. They cannot possibly be experts in every area. Consequently, many rely upon lobbyists to provide them with information about important issues. Environmental lobbyists compile information about the probable impact of various measures on the environment and are sometimes invited by legislators to help them draft new bills.

THE JOB

Environmental lobbyists strive to influence legislators and government officials through both direct and indirect lobbying. Direct lobbying involves reaching legislators themselves. Environmental lobbyists meet with members of Congress, their staff members, and other members of government. They call government officials to discuss the impact various measures might have on the environment. They sometimes testify before congressional committees or state legislatures. They distribute letters and fact sheets to legislators' offices. They sometimes try to approach legislators as they travel to and from their offices, and some lobbyists ask legislators who share their views to broach issues with other, less sympathetic legislators.

In another form of direct lobbying, environmental lobbyists strive to persuade members of Congress to serve as cosponsors for bills the lobbyists support. When a member of Congress becomes a cosponsor of a bill, his or her name is added to the list of members supporting that measure. Lobbyists typically assume that cosponsors will vote to support the bill. They also use the list of cosponsors to influence other members of Congress to support a measure. A bill's chances of one day becoming a law dramatically improve as more members agree to serve as cosponsors.

Indirect lobbying, also called grassroots lobbying, involves educating and motivating the public. The goal of indirect lobbying is to encourage members of the public to urge their representatives to vote for or against certain legislation. Environmental lobbyists use an array of indirect techniques. They issue press releases about pending legislation, hoping to inspire members of the media to write topical articles. They mail letters to citizens, urging them to write or call their representatives. They post information on the Internet and sometimes go door-to-door with information to mobilize members of environmental groups. On rare occasions, they take concerned citizens to state capitals or to Washington, D.C., to meet with representatives.

For both direct and indirect lobbying efforts, environmental lobbyists try to form coalitions with other environmental groups. Members of these coalitions work together because they have a common interest in protecting the environment. By pooling information and resources, members of the coalition can be more effective in reaching the public and members of government.

Some environmental lobbyists also support political candidates who are likely to support measures that protect the environment. They promote these candidates by distributing positive information to the public and by raising money for their campaigns.

There is a huge range of environmental issues that are brought before local, state, and federal governments every year. Clean air and water, global warming, genetic modification of crops, renewable energy, wildlife preservation, and conservation of natural resources are just a few of the major issues. A national environmental organization might lobby the federal government for tighter restrictions on air and water pollution or for laws to prohibit building or mining in an area that is a habitat of an endangered species. State and local lobbyists might propose laws to prohibit a particular company from dumping chemical waste into a specific river, offer tax credits for "green" buildings (buildings that use a minimum of nonrenewable energy and produce a minimum of pollution), or provide funds for the cleanup of neighborhoods in decline.

REQUIREMENTS

No one academic path leads directly to a lobbying career. Most lobbyists come to the profession from other disciplines and other jobs. Some have political experience, others have scientific, economic, or legal backgrounds. This previous experience can be extremely useful to environmental lobbyists, who must be able to assess the environmental and economic impact and to identify the legal strengths or weaknesses of various measures.

High School
The best way to prepare for this field is by pursuing a well-rounded education. You should, of course, study civics and history to gain an understanding of our country's political system. You also should take biology, ecology, and chemistry in order to learn about the scientific issues behind environmental legislation.

In addition to understanding politics and science, lobbyists must have a number of very practical skills, including the ability to use computers and the ability to write and speak clearly. You should, therefore, take computer courses, speech classes, and English.

Postsecondary Training
While there are no specific requirements for environmental lobbyists, most have college degrees; a growing number also have advanced degrees, particularly in political science or law.

During your undergraduate studies, you should continue to take courses that will help you understand the complex issues behind legislation and gain the practical skills that will make you an effective lobbyist. You should take courses in environmental science, geography, and geology. You should also study political science and history, which will help you understand how our political system developed and help you prepare to function within that system. Finally, study economics, because lobbyists must be able to assess the probable economic impact of pending legislation.

Lobbyists must be able to do more than understand the issues—they must also be able to write and speak about them. They must be able to influence the way other people think about issues. Communication, public relations, and English are all helpful courses for the future environmental lobbyist.

If you choose to pursue an advanced degree, you will find that having special areas of expertise, such as ecology, economics, or law, coupled with broad undergraduate backgrounds, will help you find interesting positions.

Consider serving as an intern for environmental organizations. Some colleges and universities award academic credits for internship experiences. Internships can also help you gain hands-on experience, learn about the issues, and meet potential employers. Serving as interns, says Cindy Shogan, an environmental lobbyist for the Southern Utah Wilderness Alliance, "can help students decide what they want to do within the environmental movement. It gives them a better idea of the options. It also helps them learn about other environmental organizations, so they can decide which ones appeal most to them philosophically."

Political or government experience is also invaluable for would-be lobbyists. Try to land a staff position within a legislator's office or pursue government internships. Several agencies in Washington, D.C., offer government internships. Among these are the Library of Congress, the U.S. Department of Agriculture, and the School of International Service at American University.

Certification or Licensing

Lobbyists do not need a license or certification, but are required to register. The Lobbying Disclosure Act of 1995 requires all lobbyists working on the federal level to register with the Secretary of the Senate and the Clerk of the House. You may also be required to register with the states in which you lobby and possibly pay a small fee. There is no union available to lobbyists. Some lobbyists join the American League of Lobbyists, which provides a variety of support services for its members. Membership in a number of other associations, including the American Society of Association Executives and the American Association of Political Consultants, can also be useful to lobbyists.

Sprawl

A popular issue among environmental groups today is the prevention of "sprawl," or poorly planned and much-too-rapid development of land. Sprawl leads to more traffic, decreased natural resources, increased taxes and pollution, and a lack of open space.

The Sierra Club, a prominent environmental organization, has enacted a campaign to prevent the effects of sprawl. The following are some of the components of the plan:

- enacting growth boundaries to save some land from ever being developed

- planning pedestrian-friendly development, where people have a variety of public transportation options

- saving taxpayers' money by having developers pay some of the fees for new roads, schools, water, and sewage lines

- preventing new development in disaster-prone areas such as flood-plains and coastal areas

Source: http://www.sierraclub.org

Other Requirements

Environmental lobbyists must be tenacious, self-motivated individuals. You must have excellent communications skills, be able to work well in teams, and perform well under pressure. You must understand the political process. Because lobbyists must be able to approach government officials and powerful legislators, they should be confident and outgoing. Most importantly, environmental lobbyists must be committed to protecting the environment.

"Environmental lobbyists," says Shogan, "have to be able to think quickly on their feet. If one approach isn't working, they have to be able to shift gears. They have to be flexible. They also have to have a keen strategic sense. They have to be able to look at all the angles and really think through a course of action."

According to Kevin Kirchner, an environmental lobbyist for Earthjustice Legal Defense Fund, a sense of humor can be a vital tool for an environmental lobbyist. "This is high stress work," he explains. "It's easy to get frustrated. You've got to be able to find humor in what's going on. I also think environmental lobbyists must have an unwavering dedication to accuracy and the truth. Legislators will only listen to lobbyists who have credibility."

EXPLORING

You can gain valuable practical experience by volunteering with an environmental organization. This practical experience can help you understand the issues and obstacles that environmental lobbyists encounter. By volunteering to work for local political campaigns or by serving as a page in Congress, you can learn about our country's political system. If you really feel this career might be for you, try landing an internship with an environmental organization or government agency.

EMPLOYERS

Many of our country's most respected environmental protection organizations employ environmental lobbyists. The Nature Conservancy, Sierra Club, National Wildlife Federation, Wilderness Society, and Friends of the Earth are just a few of the organizations that are actively involved in lobbying on behalf of our environment.

STARTING OUT

Students interested in becoming environmental lobbyists should contact various environmental organizations to discuss lobbying activities.

ADVANCEMENT

Environmental lobbyists can advance by gaining experience, demonstrating their abilities, or earning advanced degrees. In large environmental organizations, they also may encounter opportunities to assume management responsibilities.

Unlike lobbyists who work for special interest groups that represent major industries, environmental lobbyists are rarely motivated by ambition. Most choose the profession out of a genuine desire to protect our country's natural resources.

EARNINGS

Environmental lobbyists usually work for not-for-profit organizations with extremely limited budgets. Consequently, their salaries tend to be much lower than those of other lobbyists. While most lobbyists may earn anywhere from $12,000 to $700,000, depending on the groups they represent and their years of experience, environmental lobbyists are more likely to earn between $12,000 and $80,000.

"I would be shocked," says Cindy Shogan, "to learn that any of my colleagues were earning more than $80,000."

Kevin Kirchner comments, "Environmental lobbyists must have an enormous commitment on a personal level because they just don't get paid as much as they could in other jobs and they often work longer hours."

WORK ENVIRONMENT

Because most environmental lobbyists work for not-for-profit organizations, they often have limited staff and even more limited budgets. Consequently, environmental lobbyists usually combine highly professional skills, such as scientific or legal expertise, with clerical capabilities. In other words, environmental lobbyists must be willing to stuff envelopes as well as meet with senators.

According to Cindy Shogan, lobbyists' schedules are determined by Congress's schedule. "If Congress is on break," she says, "people dress more casually and spend time catching up on research, paperwork, and grassroots lobbying. When Congress is in session, you're in constant crisis mode." Crisis mode for an environmental lobbyist entails 12- and 14-hour days, irregular hours, and frequent trips to Capitol Hill.

Environmental lobbyists often face frustrating setbacks. Measures they support can take years to wend their way through Congress. Along the way, they can be altered and weakened almost beyond recognition. This can be stressful and disappointing, but environmental lobbyists must be able to put these feelings aside and move on to the next challenge.

OUTLOOK

Regrettably, there is no shortage of environmental concerns in our country. As long as people continue to pollute our air and water, cut down forests, develop land, and mine the earth, environmental groups will continue to fight for legislation that will protect our natural resources. This profession is, therefore, expected to grow about as fast as the average through 2010.

The nation's economy can affect environmental protection organizations, which are largely funded by donations. During recessions, people may not be able to give as generously to not-for-profit organizations. Environmental protection organizations may, in turn, be forced to cut back on their lobbying efforts.

The nation's administration also affects the work of environmental lobbyists and the organizations or causes they represent. Some administrations are more sensitive to environmental issues. For example the George W. Bush administration is generally considered weak on environmental issues. It has come under criticism on several environmental issues, including the rejection of the Kyoto Protocol on global warming, the proposal to drill for oil in protected areas of the Arctic National Wildlife Refuge in Alaska, and overturning a ruling to reduce arsenic levels in drinking water by 80 percent.

FOR MORE INFORMATION

For career information, contact
   American League of Lobbyists
   PO Box 30005
   Alexandria, VA 22310
   Tel: 703-960-3011
   Email: info@alldc.org
   http://www.alldc.org/

ECO provides career information, publications, and internship information, among many other services.
   Environmental Careers Organization (ECO)
   179 South Street
   Boston, MA 02111
   Tel: 617-426-4375
   http://www.eco.org/

Environmental Technicians

QUICK FACTS

School Subjects
Biology
Chemistry

Personal Skills
Mechanical/manipulative
Technical/scientific

Work Environment
Indoors and outdoors
One location with some
  travel

Minimum Education Level
Some postsecondary training

Salary Range
$17,483 to $33,821 to
  $50,000+

Certification or Licensing
Required for certain
  positions

Outlook
About as fast as the average

DOT
029

GOE
05.03.08

NOC
2231

O*NET-SOC
19-2041.00, 19-4091.00

OVERVIEW

Environmental technicians, also known as *pollution control technicians*, conduct tests and field investigations to obtain soil samples and other data. Their research is used by engineers, scientists, and others who help clean up, monitor, control, or prevent pollution. An environmental technician usually specializes in air, water, or soil pollution. Although work differs by employer and specialty, technicians generally collect samples for laboratory analysis, using specialized instruments and equipment, monitor pollution control devices and systems, such as smokestack air "scrubbers," and perform various other tests and investigations to evaluate pollution problems. They follow strict procedures in collecting and recording data in order to meet the requirements of environmental laws.

In general, environmental technicians do not operate the equipment and systems designed to prevent pollution or remove pollutants. Instead, they test environmental conditions. In addition, some analyze and report on their findings.

There are approximately 27,000 environmental science and protection technicians, including health technicians, in the United States.

HISTORY

Stricter pollution control regulations of the mid-1960s to early 1970s created a job market for environmental technicians. As regulations on industry have become more stringent, the job has grown both in number and in scope. For centuries, the biosphere (the self-regulating "envelope" of air, water, and land in which all life on Earth exists) was generally able to scatter, break down, or adapt to all the wastes and pollution produced by people.

This began to change drastically with the industrial revolution. Beginning in England in the 1750s, the industrial revolution caused the shift from a farming society to an industrialized society. Although it had many economic benefits, it took a terrible toll on the environment. Textile manufacturing and iron processing spread through England, and coal-powered mills, machines, and factories spewed heavy black smoke into the air. Rivers and lakes became open sewers as factories dumped their wastes anywhere. By the 19th century, areas with high population density and clusters of factories were experiencing markedly higher death and disease rates than areas with little industrial development.

As the industrial revolution spread across the world, there were warning signs that the biosphere could not handle the resulting pollution. Smog hung over large cities with many factories. Residents experienced more respiratory and other health problems. Manufacturing wastes and untreated sewage poisoned surface waters and underground sources of water, affecting water supplies and increasing disease. Wastes and pollution also seeped into soil, affecting crops.

After World War II, the development of new synthetic materials and their resulting waste products, including plastics, pesticides, and vehicle exhaust that are difficult to degrade (break down) worsened pollution problems. Fish and wildlife were dying because rivers and lakes were choked with chemicals and wastes. Scientists documented connections between pollution and birth defects, cancer, fertility problems, genetic damage, and many other serious problems.

Not until the mid-1960s to early 1970s did public outcry, environmental activism, and political and economic necessity force the passage of stricter pollution-control laws. Federal environmental legislation mandated cleanups of existing air, water, and soil pollution, and began to limit the type and amount of polluting substances that industry could release to the environment. Manufacturers were required to operate within stricter guidelines for air emissions, wastewater treatment and disposal, and other polluting activities. States and municipalities also were given increasing responsibilities for monitoring and working to reduce levels of auto, industrial, and other pollution. Out of the need to meet these new requirements, the pollution control industry was born—and with it, the job of environmental technician.

THE JOB

Environmental technicians usually specialize in one aspect of pollution control, such as water pollution, air pollution, or soil pollution. Sampling, monitoring, and testing are the major activities of the job. No matter what the specialty, environmental technicians work largely for or with government agencies that regulate pollution by industry.

Increasingly, technicians input their data into computers. Instruments used to collect water samples or monitor water sources may be highly sophisticated electronic devices. Technicians usually do not analyze the data they collect. However, they may report on what they know to scientists or engineers, either verbally or in writing.

Water pollution technicians monitor both industrial and residential discharge, such as from wastewater treatment plants. They help to determine the presence and extent of pollutants in water. They collect samples from lakes, streams, rivers, groundwater, industrial or municipal wastewater, or other sources. Samples are brought to labs, where chemical and other tests are performed. If the samples contain harmful substances, remedial (cleanup) actions will need to be taken. These technicians also may perform various field tests, such as checking the pH, oxygen, and nitrate level of surface waters.

Some water pollution technicians set up monitoring equipment to obtain information on water flow, movement, temperature, or pressure and record readings from these devices. To trace flow patterns, they may inject dyes into the water.

Technicians have to be careful not to contaminate their samples, stray from the specific testing procedure, or otherwise do something to ruin the sample or cause faulty or misleading results.

Depending on the specific job, water pollution technicians may spend a good part of their time outdoors, in good weather and bad, aboard boats, and sometimes near unpleasant smells or potentially hazardous substances. Field sites may be in remote areas. In some cases, the technician may have to fly to a different part of the country, perhaps staying away from home for a long period of time.

Water pollution technicians play a big role in industrial wastewater discharge monitoring, treatment, and control. Some technicians specialize in groundwater, ocean water, or other types of natural waters. *Estuarine resource technicians,* for example, specialize in estuary waters, or coastal areas where fresh water and salt water come together. These bays, salt marshes, inlets, and other tidal water bodies support a wide variety of plant and animal life with ecologically complex relationships. They are vulnerable to destructive pollution from adjoining industries, cities and towns, and other sources. Estuarine resource technicians aid scientists in studying the resulting environmental changes. They may work in laboratories or aboard boats, or may use diving gear to collect samples directly.

Air pollution technicians collect and test air samples (for example, from chimneys of industrial manufacturing plants), record data on atmospheric conditions (such as determining levels of airborne substances from auto or industrial emissions), and supply data to scientists and engineers for further testing and analysis. In labs, air pollution technicians may help test air samples or re-create contaminants. They may use atomic absorption spectrophotometers, flame photometers, gas chromatographs, and other instruments for analyzing samples.

In the field, air pollution technicians may use rooftop sampling devices or operate mobile monitoring units or stationary trailers. The trailers may be equipped with elaborate automatic testing systems, including some of the same devices found in laboratories. Outside air is pumped into various chambers in the trailer where it is analyzed for the presence of pollutants. The results can be recorded by machine on 30-day rolls of graph paper or fed into a computer at regular intervals. Technicians set up and maintain the sampling devices, replenish the chemicals used in tests, replace worn parts, calibrate instruments, and record results. Some air pollution technicians specialize in certain pollutants or pollution sources. For example, *engine emission technicians* focus on exhaust from internal combustion engines.

Soil or land pollution technicians collect soil, silt, or mud samples and check them for contamination. Soil can become contaminated when polluted water seeps into the earth, such as when liquid waste leaks from a landfill or other source into surrounding ground. Soil pollution technicians work for federal, state, and local government agencies, for private consulting firms, and elsewhere. (Some soil conservation technicians perform pollution control work.)

A position sometimes grouped with other environmental technicians is that of *noise pollution technician*. Noise pollution technicians use rooftop devices and mobile units to take readings and collect data on noise levels of factories, highways, airports, and other locations in order to determine noise exposure levels for workers or the public. Some test noise levels of construction equipment, chainsaws, snow blowers, lawn mowers, or other equipment.

REQUIREMENTS

High School

In high school, key courses include biology, chemistry, and physics. Conservation or ecology courses also will be useful, if your school offers them. Math classes should include at least algebra and geometry, and taking English and speech classes will help to sharpen your communications skills. In addition, work on developing your computer skills while in high school, either on your own or through a class.

Postsecondary Training

Some technician positions call for a high school degree plus employer training. As environmental work becomes more technical and complex, more positions are being filled by technicians with at least an associate's degree. To meet this need, many community colleges across the country have developed appropriate programs for environmental technicians. Areas of study include environmental engineering technologies, pollution control technologies, conservation, and ecology. Courses include meteorology, toxicology, source testing, sampling, and analysis, air quality management, environmental science, and statistics. Other training requirements vary by employer. Some experts advise attending school in the part of the country where you'd like to begin your career so you can start getting to know local employers before you graduate.

Certification or Licensing

Certification or licensing is required for some positions in pollution control, especially those in which sanitation, public health, a public water supply, or a sewage treatment system is involved. For example, the Institute of Professional Environmental Practice offers the Qualified Environmental Professional (QEP) and the Environmental Professional Intern (EPI) certifications. See the end of this article for contact information.

Other Requirements

Environmental technicians should be curious, patient, detail-oriented, and capable of following instructions. Basic manual skills are a must for collecting samples and performing similar tasks. Complex environmental regulations drive technicians' jobs; therefore, it's crucial that they are able to read and understand technical materials and to carefully follow any written guidelines for sampling or other procedures. Computer skills and the ability to read and interpret maps, charts, and diagrams are also necessary.

Technicians must make accurate and objective observations, maintain clear and complete records, and be exact in their computations. In addition, good physical conditioning is a requirement for some activities, for example, climbing up smokestacks to take emission samples.

EXPLORING

To learn more about environmental jobs, visit your local library and read some technical and general-interest publications in environmental science. This might give you an idea of the technologies being used and issues being discussed in the field today. You also can visit a municipal health department or pollution control agency in your community. Many agencies are pleased to explain their work to visitors.

School science clubs, local community groups, and naturalist clubs may help broaden your understanding of various aspects of the natural world and give you some experience. Most schools have recycling programs that enlist student help.

With the help of a teacher or career counselor, a tour of a local manufacturing plant using an air- or water-pollution abatement system also might be arranged. Many plants offer tours of their operations to the public. This would provide an excellent opportunity to see technicians at work.

As a high school student, it may be difficult to obtain summer or part-time work as a technician due to the extensive operations and safety training required for some of these jobs. However, it is worthwhile to check with a local environmental agency, nonprofit environmental organizations, or private consulting firms to learn of volunteer or paid support opportunities. Any hands-on experience you can get will be of value to a future employer.

EMPLOYERS

Many jobs for environmental technicians are with the government agencies that monitor the environment, such as the Environmental Protection Agency (EPA), and the Departments of Agriculture, Energy, and Interior.

Water pollution technicians may be employed by manufacturers that produce wastewater, municipal wastewater treatment facilities, private firms hired to monitor or control pollutants in water or wastewater, and government regulatory agencies responsible for protecting water quality.

Air pollution technicians work for government agencies such as regional EPA offices. They also work for private manufacturers producing airborne pollutants, research facilities, pollution control equipment manufacturers, and other employers.

Soil pollution technicians may work for federal or state departments of agriculture and EPA offices. They also work for private agricultural groups that monitor soil quality for pesticide levels.

Noise pollution technicians are employed by private companies and by government agencies such as OSHA (Occupational Safety and Health Administration).

STARTING OUT

Graduates of two-year environmental programs are often employed during their final term by recruiters who visit their schools. Specific opportunities will vary depending on the part of the country, the segment of the environmental industry, the specialization of the technician (air, water, or land), the economy, and other factors. Many beginning technicians find the greatest number of positions available in state or local government agencies.

Most schools provide job-hunting advice and assistance. Direct application to state or local environmental agencies, employment agencies, or potential employers can also be a productive approach. If you hope to find employment outside your current geographic area, you may get good results by checking with professional organizations or by reading advertisements in technical journals, many of which have searchable job listings on the Internet.

ADVANCEMENT

The typical hierarchy for environmental work is technician (two years of postsecondary education or less), technologist (two years or more of postsecondary training), technician manager (perhaps a technician or technologist with many years of experience), and scientist or engineer (four-year bachelor of science degree or more, up to Ph.D. level).

In some private manufacturing or consulting firms, technician positions are used for training newly recruited professional staff. In such cases, workers with four-year degrees in engineering or physical science are likely to be promoted before those with two-year degrees. Employees of government agencies usually are organized under civil service systems that specify experience, education, and other criteria for advancement. Private industry promotions are structured differently and will depend on a variety of factors.

EARNINGS

Pay for environmental technicians varies widely depending on the nature of the work they do, training and experience required for the work, type of employer, geographic region, and other factors. Public-sector positions tend to pay less than private-sector positions.

According to the U.S. Department of Labor, median hourly earnings of environmental science and protection technicians, including health technicians, were $16.26 in 2000. Government entry-level salaries for environmental technicians ranged from $17,483 to $22,251 per year, depending on education and experience. Technicians who become managers or supervisors can earn up to $50,000 per year or more. Technicians who work in private industry or who further their education to secure teaching positions can also expect to earn higher than average salaries.

No matter which area they specialize in, environmental technicians generally enjoy fringe benefits such as paid vacation, holidays and sick time, and employer-paid training. Technicians who work full time (and some who work part time) often have health insurance benefits. Technicians who are employed by the federal government may get additional benefits, such as pension and retirement benefits.

WORK ENVIRONMENT

Conditions range from clean and pleasant indoor offices and laboratories to hot, cold, wet, bad-smelling, noisy, or even hazardous settings outdoors. Anyone planning a career in environmental technology should realize the possibility of exposure to unpleasant conditions at least occasionally in his or her career. Employers often can minimize these negatives through special equipment and procedures. Most laboratories and manufacturing companies have safety procedures for potentially dangerous situations.

Some jobs involve vigorous physical activity, such as handling a small boat or climbing a tall ladder. For the most part, technicians need only to be prepared for moderate activity. Travel may be required; technicians go to urban, industrial, or rural settings for sampling.

Because their job can involve a considerable amount of repetitive work, patience and the ability to handle routine are important. Yet, particularly when environmental technicians are working in the field, they also have to be ready to use their resourcefulness and ingenuity to find the best ways of responding to new situations.

OUTLOOK

Demand for environmental technicians is expected to increase about as fast as the average through 2010. Those trained to handle increasingly complex technical demands will have the upper hand. Environmental technicians will be needed to regulate waste products; to collect air, water, and soil samples for measuring levels of pollutants; to monitor compliance with environmental regulations; and to clean up contaminated sites.

Demand will be higher in some areas of the country than others depending on specialty; for example, air pollution technicians will be especially in demand in large cities, such as Los Angeles and New York, which face pressure to comply with national air quality standards. Amount of industrialization, stringency of state and local pollution control enforcement, health of local economy, and other factors also will affect demand by region and specialty. Perhaps one of the greatest factors affecting environmental work is continued mandates for pollution control by the federal government. As long as the federal government is supporting pollution control, the environmental technician will be needed.

FOR MORE INFORMATION

For job listings and certification information, contact
Air and Waste Management Association
420 Fort Duquesne Boulevard
One Gateway Center, Third Floor
Pittsburgh, PA 15222
Tel: 412-232-3444
Email: info@awma.org
http://www.awma.org

For information on the engineering field and technician certification, contact
American Society of Certified Engineering Technicians
PO Box 1348
Flowery Branch, GA 30542
Tel: 770-967-9173
http://www.ascet.org

The following organization is an environmental careers resource for high school and college students.
Environmental Careers Organization
179 South Street
Boston, MA 02111
Tel: 617-426-4375
http://www.eco.org

For information on environmental careers and student employment opportunities, contact
Environmental Protection Agency
Ariel Rios Building
1200 Pennsylvania Ave, NW
Washington, DC 20460
Tel: 202-260-2090
http://www.epa.gov

For information on certification, contact
Institute of Professional Environmental Practice
600 Forbes Avenue
333 Fisher Hall
Pittsburgh, PA 15282
Tel: 412-396-1703
Email: ipep@duq.edu
http://www.ipep.org

For job listings and scholarship opportunities, contact
National Ground Water Association
601 Dempsey Road
Westerville, OH 43081-8978
Tel: 800-551-7379
Email: ngwa@ngwa.org
http://www.ngwa.org

For information on conferences and workshops, contact
Water Environment Federation
601 Wythe Street
Alexandria, VA 22314-1994
Tel: 800-666-0206
http://www.wef.org

Fish and Game Wardens

QUICK FACTS

School Subjects
Biology
Earth science

Personal Skills
Helping/teaching
Leadership/management

Work Environment
Primarily outdoors
Primarily multiple locations

Minimum Education Level
Bachelor's degree

Salary Range
$18,000 to $35,519 to
$91,000

Certification or Licensing
Required for certain
positions

Outlook
About as fast as the average

DOT
379

GOE
04.01.02

NOC
2224

O*NET-SOC
33-3031.00

OVERVIEW

Professional wildlife conservationists, once widely known as *fish and game wardens*, are now known by a variety of titles. Jobs falling under this category in the federal government include *U.S. Fish and Wildlife Service special agents, federal law enforcement officers, wildlife inspectors, refuge rangers*, and *refuge officers*. On a state or municipal level, the job title might be *conservation police, environmental conservation police*, or *conservation wardens*. Along with the job title, the job itself has expanded. Once, the fish and game warden was hired solely to protect wildlife. Today, in addition to that original responsibility, they perform a wide variety of tasks related to resource management, public information, and law enforcement. Approximately 7,500 people are employed by the U.S. Fish and Wildlife Service.

HISTORY

For centuries, wildlife has suffered because of the actions of human beings. Increasingly efficient weapons made it easier for people to kill game. ("Game" may be broadly defined as any fish, birds, or mammals that are hunted noncommercially for food, sport, or both.) Some species of animals have been hunted to extinction. Forests have been cleared, swamps drained, and rivers dammed to clear the way for agriculture and industry. These activities have harmed or destroyed large areas of plant and wildlife habitat.

Beginning in the late 19th century, growing concern for vanishing wildlife led to the initiation of comprehensive conservation actions. The governments of the United States and other nations have since passed protective laws and set aside national parks and other reserves for wildlife.

The principal agency assigned to the conservation and enhancement of animals and their habitats in this country is the U.S. Fish and Wildlife Service. An agency of the U.S. Department of the Interior, it is responsible for the scientific development of commercial fisheries and the conservation of fish and wildlife. The service, which was created in 1856, manages the 93 million-acre National Wildlife Refuge System. This system includes 520 National Wildlife Refuges, thousands of smaller wetlands, and other special management areas. It also operates 66 National Fish Hatcheries, 64 fishery resource offices, and 78 ecological services field stations.

THE JOB

The conservation of fish and wildlife is a responsibility that grows more complex each year, especially with growing pollution and environmental changes. To accomplish its mission, the U.S. Fish and Wildlife Service employs many of the country's best biologists, wildlife managers, engineers, realty specialists, law enforcement agents, and others. These individuals perform a variety of tasks, such as saving endangered and threatened species, conserving migratory birds and inland fisheries, providing expert advice to other federal agencies, industry, and foreign governments, and managing nearly 700 offices and field stations. These personnel work in every state and territory from the Arctic Ocean to the South Pacific, and from the Atlantic to the Caribbean.

Wildlife inspectors and special agents are two job titles that have arisen from "fish and game wardens." *Wildlife inspectors* monitor the legal trade and intercept illegal importations and exportations of federally protected fish and wildlife. At points of entry into the United States, wildlife inspectors examine shipping containers, live animals, wildlife products such as animal skins, and documents. Inspectors, who work closely with special agents, may seize shipments as evidence, conduct investigations, and testify in courts of law.

Special agents of the U.S. Fish and Wildlife Service are trained criminal investigators who enforce federal wildlife laws throughout this country. Special agents conduct law enforcement investigations, which may include activities such as surveillance, undercover work,

A fish and game warden drives an airboat over swamps near Miami, Florida, on a routine patrol. (*Corbis*)

making arrests, and preparing cases for court. They often work with other federal, tribal, foreign, state, or local law enforcement authorities. These agents enforce traditional migratory bird regulations and investigate commercial activities involving illegal trade in protected wildlife. Some agents work at border ports to enforce federal laws protecting wildlife that enters into interstate and national commerce.

Another prominent position within the Fish and Wildlife Service is that of a *refuge ranger* or *refuge manager*. These professionals work at 520 national refuges across the country, protecting and conserving migratory and native species of birds, mammals, fish, endangered species, and other wildlife. Many of these refuges also offer outdoor recreational opportunities and programs to educate the public about the refuges' wildlife and their habitats.

Judie Miller is a refuge ranger and public affairs officer at the Minnesota Valley National Wildlife Refuge, located in Bloomington, Minnesota. She is responsible for outreach at the refuge, "which means that I need to inform not only the public, but our internal audiences about our mission and what we are doing."

Miller notes that "refuge ranger" is a pretty generic title. "Some of our rangers work in law enforcement; some are environmental educators and interpreters; some work in public affairs or as volunteer officers. These are some of the functional jobs within the generic category. My job also includes handling a number of special events at Minnesota Valley. For example, I coordinate the National Wildlife Refuge Week events at this refuge. I do many other outreach jobs—such as creating and writing newsletters, press releases, etc., to get word out to people about our refuge."

The U.S. Fish and Wildlife Service also employs people in a wide variety of occupations, such as engineering, ecology, zoology, veterinary science, forestry, botany, chemistry, hydrology, land surveying, architecture, landscape architecture, statistics, library science, archaeology, education, and guidance counseling. The service hires administrators and business managers, realty specialists, appraisers, assessors, contract specialists, purchasing agents, budget analysts, financial managers, computer specialists and programmers, human resources professionals, and public affairs specialists. Additionally, a variety of technical, clerical, and trades and crafts positions are available.

REQUIREMENTS

High School

It is advisable for high school students interested in a career in this field to take courses in biology and other sciences, geography, mathematics, social studies, and physical education. Judie Miller recommends that you look for cooperative programs available at some high schools and colleges; these programs allow you to study as well as work in programs at refuges and other facilities—and in some cases, get paid for some of the hours you work at the facility.

Postsecondary Training

All positions in this category require a bachelor's degree or three years of work-related experience. Higher positions require at least one year of graduate studies; as you move up the scale to increasingly professional positions, master's or even doctoral degrees become mandatory.

Specialized positions require advanced education or training. For example, all biology-related positions require a bachelor's degree in biology, or a combination of education and experience equivalent to a degree that includes an appropriate number of semester hours in biological science.

Additional on-the-job training is given for most positions. Special agents are given 18 weeks of formal training in criminal investigative and wildlife law enforcement techniques at the Federal Law Enforcement Training Center in Glynco, Georgia.

Other Requirements

Some positions have physical fitness and ability requirements, so you must undergo a battery of physical tests. To qualify for a special agent position, you must meet strict medical, physical, and psychological requirements. You must also participate in mandatory drug testing and psychological screening programs.

Only the most highly qualified candidates will be interviewed for special agent positions. Those chosen undergo extensive background investigations to determine suitability for appointment. All special agent appointees must be citizens of the United States and between 21 and 37 years of age when entering. Additionally, you must sign a mobility agreement, which indicates a willingness to accept a reassignment to any location in the future.

It is important to bear in mind that fish and game wardens don't just work with fish and game. They spend a lot of time working with other officials and with members of the general public. Therefore, they must have good communication skills and enjoy working with people as much as animals.

EXPLORING

Doing volunteer work at a fish and wildlife facility is a good way to get some experience in this field and to determine whether you would like to pursue a career in the area. Of course, it would be ideal to volunteer for the U.S. Fish and Wildlife Service, but serving with other environmental organizations can be very useful as well. College students—and even students at select high schools—can apply for formal internships with various wildlife agencies. These can usually provide college (or possibly high school) credit and may even pay a small stipend.

EMPLOYERS

The largest number of jobs in the field is found with the U.S. Fish and Wildlife Service and other agencies of the Department of the Interior, such as the National Park Service. Individual states also have positions in this area; contact your local state government, especially your state's park association. In Illinois, for example, you might contact the Illinois Department of Natural Resources.

STARTING OUT

The U.S. Fish and Wildlife Service fills jobs in various ways, including promoting or reassigning current employees, transferring employees from other federal agencies, rehiring former federal employees, or hiring applicants from outside the federal service. Some summer jobs are also filled by hiring applicants. Applications for these positions must be submitted during a specified period—usually sometime between January and April of each year. The number and types of temporary positions vary from year to year. Contact the regional office nearest you to learn about current opportunities.

For information about specific Fish and Wildlife Service job openings, contact the Office of Personnel Management in your area. Your telephone directory will list the number and address of the office nearest you (under U.S. Government). Career planning and placement directors at colleges and universities can supply career information and training opportunities. Also, state employment or job services offices maintain listings of federal position vacancies. These offices can help you obtain the necessary forms to apply for jobs or direct you to sources for additional information.

A great way to check job listings is over the Internet, where you can access USAJOBS (http://www.usajobs.opm.gov), a job bank for the U.S. government.

ADVANCEMENT

Prospects for advancement in this field improve greatly if fish and game wardens are willing to relocate. While they certainly can be promoted within their own facility, relocation opens up the possibility of taking a higher position whenever one opens up at any U.S. Fish and Wildlife Service location around the country.

EARNINGS

Like all federal employees, those who work for the U.S. Fish and Wildlife Service earn salaries as prescribed by law. Service employees are classified either as "general schedule" (GS) or as "wage grade" (WG). General schedule employees, the professional, technical, administrative, and clerical workers, receive annual salaries based on their GS grades 1 through 15. GS-5 salaries in 2003 ranged from $23,442 to $30,471. GS-7 salaries ranged from $29,037 to $37,749. GS-9 salaries ranged from $35,519 to $46,175. There are some areas in the United States. that have an additional geographic locality pay.

In the wide variety of positions available at the U.S. Fish and Wildlife Service, salaries range from $18,000 all the way up to $91,000 for more advanced positions. Law enforcement positions, especially special agents, receive higher salaries because of the danger inherent in their jobs.

WORK ENVIRONMENT

With a number of different positions available, the work environment for each, of course, varies substantially. Wildlife inspectors, conservation police, or special agents generally spend a great deal of time outdoors, sometimes in remote areas, perhaps pursuing wildlife criminals. Yet they also need to spend time indoors, preparing detailed reports of their investigations and seeking additional information by searching on their computers.

A refuge ranger or manager will divide work time between indoor and outdoor activities. The various types of biologists will also spend time both indoors and outdoors, as their particular job dictates. All of these employees, however, will have a passion for the land and animal life, a dedication to preserving our environment, and the desire to make a difference in effecting positive changes. It can be very rewarding work in terms of personal satisfaction and sense of accomplishment. Very few of these jobs are of the nine-to-five variety, though; most require putting in extra hours.

OUTLOOK

As with any career with the government, growth potential depends a lot on the political scene and what the views are of those in power, whether on a national or local level. However, as Judie Miller says, there is "lots of work to be done and people are becoming more and more concerned about environmental issues. We need to have good water, good places to play and swim and hunt and fish. Jobs are always available, but the number depends on the political situation at a given time."

FOR MORE INFORMATION

To learn more about fish and game wardens and related employment opportunities, contact the following organizations:

U.S. Fish and Wildlife Service
Department of the Interior
1849 C Street, NW
Washington, DC 20240
Tel: 703-358-2120
http://www.fws.gov

U.S. National Park Service
Department of the Interior
1849 C Street, NW
Washington, DC 20240
Tel: 202-208-6843
http://www.nps.gov

Foresters

QUICK FACTS

School Subjects
Earth science
English
Mathematics

Personal Skills
Helping/teaching
Leadership/management
Technical/scientific

Work Environment
Indoors and outdoors
Primarily one location

Minimum Education Level
Bachelor's degree

Salary Range
$23,776 to $43,640 to
$65,960+

Certification or Licensing
Required for certain states

Outlook
More slowly than the average

DOT
040

GOE
03.01.04

NOC
2122

O*NET-SOC
19-1032.00, 45-4011.00

OVERVIEW

Foresters protect and manage forest resources, one of our greatest natural assets, through various biological techniques. Using their specialized knowledge of tree biology and ecology, wood science, and manufacturing processes, they manage forests for timber production, protect them from fire and pest damage, harvest mature forests, and re-establish new forests after harvesting. Foresters and conservation scientists hold about 29,000 jobs in the United States.

HISTORY

Not so long ago, forests were considered a hindrance to farming, a barrier to settlement, and a surplus commodity of minimal value to a small population of settlers. No profession existed to protect and manage the forests. As the U.S. population grew and land clearing increased in the mid-19th century, however, people with foresight realized that forests were becoming more valuable and, unless protected, might disappear entirely. Laws enacted by the federal and state governments around that time helped to slow down forest destruction. At the same time, opening the western territories to farming allowed forests to reclaim marginal farms abandoned in the East.

In 1900, seven individuals founded the Society of American Foresters (SAF). At that time, they embodied practically the whole profession of forestry. By 1905, the U.S. Forest Service was established within the Department of Agriculture. Two years later, the

Forest Service assumed responsibility for managing the newly established national forests.

Today, there are 155 national forests and 20 grasslands. Each forest is divided into ranger districts, of which there are more than 600. Each district is run by a staff of 10–100 people, depending on the district's size. Not all of the country's forested land, however, is owned by the federal government. Many forest lands are owned by states and municipalities, and more than 50 percent of the country's forested land is privately owned. These nonfederally owned forest areas amount to approximately 500 million acres and account for about 20 percent of the country's land mass. Because of the growing awareness that forest resources need to be managed wisely, the forestry profession has developed rapidly. Foresters and forestry technicians are charged with protecting the nation's forests from fire, insects, and diseases; managing them for wood crops, water, wildlife, and forage; preserving their beauty and making it accessible; and training others to carry on their work.

THE JOB

Foresters do much of their work outdoors, especially during the early part of their careers. Ralph Unversaw, a district forester for Indiana, still spends most of his time outdoors. "Normally, I spend about four days out of a five-day workweek outside, and the fifth inside trying to catch up on paperwork," he says. Most of Unversaw's job involves working with private woodland owners to manage their properties. "My job is to promote forest management," he says. "If they want to do some sort of timber management, I can advise them on planting, selecting trees for harvest, and harvesting."

Beginning foresters perform many duties. They may map areas of a forest and estimate the amounts of resources, such as timber, game shelter, and food, water, and forage for cattle and sheep that they provide. They may also determine areas that need intervention, such as planting trees, scattering seed from helicopters, controlling disease or insects, thinning dense forest stands, or pruning trees to produce better lumber or plywood. They may monitor stands of trees to ensure healthy growth and determine the best time for harvesting. They may lay out logging roads or roads to lakes and recreational facilities and create the plans for building wilderness areas. Foresters may supervise crews doing all these jobs and inspect their work after it is done.

Foresters select and mark trees to be cut and check on the cutting and removal of the logs and pulpwood. They may be in charge of the lookouts, patrols, and pilots who detect fires and may lead crews that fight fires. They also sometimes oversee the operation of recreational areas, collect fees, issue permits, give talks to groups of campers, find lost hikers, and rescue climbers and skiers.

Even for foresters in the early stages of their careers, however, the work is not all outdoors. They must record the work done in the forest on maps and in reports. They use computers, data-processing equipment, and aerial photography to assist in this process. Although most beginning foresters do most of their work outside, some do work primarily indoors, in the technical laboratories and factories of wood-using industries. They may work in sawmills, plywood and hardboard plants, pulp and paper mills, wood-preserving plants, and furniture factories. These foresters are specialists in wood technology or pulp and paper technology. Many forest scientists work in laboratories and greenhouses, as well as in the forests, to learn how trees and forests grow.

When used wisely, a forest offers many benefits and can be used for several purposes. To maximize these benefits and purposes, foresters must not only know a great deal about the forest resources, but also be able to understand people, explain technical information to them, and secure their cooperation. Foresters, from the very start of their careers, can expect to be called on to speak before various groups, from elementary school classes to service clubs and meetings of scientific societies. While not all foresters are in frequent contact with the public, they all eventually discover that their advancement depends on their ability to work with other people. "In my job, I have to do a lot of public relations-type work," says Unversaw. "I provide a lot of educational programs to the public—both to youth and to adults."

Much of the work that foresters do involves the application of scientific knowledge and theory to actual practice in the field. Some foresters specialize in one or two of the basic sciences. In fact, some foresters are engaged in research that delves deeply into the fundamental physical and biological sciences. They work in laboratories with many modern techniques and devices.

The scientific knowledge of how forests live is the specialty of *silviculturists,* who practice the art of establishing or reproducing forests, regulating their makeup, and influencing their growth and development along predetermined lines. The art of silviculture and the principles of economics and finance are the foundations of forest preservation and management.

One branch of forestry, known as forest engineering or logging engineering, combines forestry and engineering. Work in this field includes the design and construction of roads, bridges, dams, and buildings in forest areas. The design, selection, and installation of equipment for moving logs and pulpwood out of the forest is the special field of the *logging,* or *forest, engineer.* Forest and logging engineers may be graduates of schools of forestry that offer courses in this specialty, or they may have been trained as civil, mechanical, or electrical engineers.

Another type of specialist, the *forest ecologist,* conducts research to find out how forests are affected by changes in environmental conditions, such as soil, light, climate, altitude, and animal populations.

Foresters use a number of tools to perform their jobs: clinometers measure the heights, diameter tapes measure the diameters, and increment borers and bark gauges measure the growth of trees. Photogrammetry and remote sensing (aerial photographs taken from airplanes and satellites) are often used for mapping large forest areas and detecting widespread trends of forest and land use. Computers are used extensively, both in the office and in the field, to store, retrieve, and analyze the information required to manage the forest land and its resources.

In most forestry organizations and groups, a great deal of physical work in the woods needs to be done. This work is usually done by people with experience and aptitude but little formal education beyond high school or by forest technicians who have graduated from one- or two-year programs in forest technicians' institutes or ranger schools.

REQUIREMENTS

In preparation for becoming a forester, Ralph Unversaw obtained a bachelor's degree in forestry and wildlife management. The minimal educational requirement to enter this career is a bachelor's degree in forestry; however, some foresters combine three years of liberal arts education with two years of professional education in forestry and receive the degrees of bachelor of arts and master of forestry. The SAF, the professional society to which most foresters belong, currently accredits more than 45 schools in the United States with programs leading to forestry degrees at the bachelor's and master's levels. These programs are found in 38 states, most of them associated with state universities. (For a listing of accredited programs, visit this section of the SAF website, http://www.safnet.org/education/pforschools.htm.)

High School

To prepare for entry into a college forestry program, you will need to specifically focus on mathematics and sciences in high school. Take algebra, geometry, and statistics as well as biology, chemistry, physics, and any science course that will teach you about ecology. English classes are also important to take since part of your job is likely to include researching, writing reports, and presenting your findings. In addition, take history, economics, and, if possible, agriculture classes, which will teach you about soils and plant growth, among other things.

Postsecondary Training

The courses of study in all accredited schools of forestry have the same fundamental components. To be accredited, a school must offer a specified amount of instruction in four essential areas of study: *forest management* (the application of business methods and silvicultural principles to the operation of forest properties), *forest ecology and biology* (ecosystem management and physiological principles including fires, insects, diseases, wildlife, and weather), *forest policy and administration* (understanding legislative procedures and environmental regulations that influence management decisions), and *forest measurements* (the inventory process for quantifying forest resources such as timber amount and quality, wildlife habitat, water quality, and recreational potential). The courses in these four topics, which are generally concentrated in the junior and senior years, make up the professional portion of the forester's schooling.

To prepare for these subjects, you need a grounding in mathematics, surveying, chemistry, physics, botany, zoology, soil science, economics, and geology. Moreover, to help develop the skills needed for self-education later in your career, you need basic courses in literature, social studies, and writing. All these courses are organized in a program that fills the freshman and sophomore years largely with basic sciences and humanities.

Foresters also do fieldwork as a part of their university training. Some schools of forestry are so close to forests that regular three-hour or all-day laboratory sessions are conducted in the school forest. Following the sophomore year in many schools of forestry is a summer camp period of eight to 11 weeks. This is basically a continuous laboratory period during which you take part in the life of the forest, and, under guidance of the faculty, store up experience on which to draw in your junior and senior professional courses. In addition, some schools of forestry require you to spend an entire summer working for a forestry organization such as the U.S. Forest Service, National Park Service, a state forest service, or a company in the forest industry. The employer usually reports back to the school on your progress.

In addition to the basic sciences and humanities and the four core forestry areas of study, elective courses are offered to enable you to specialize in such fields as forest or logging engineering, wood technology, range management, wildlife management, forest recreation, and watershed management.

Graduates of forestry schools who wish to specialize in a certain area or broaden their general knowledge of forestry or related fields may opt for graduate work at one of the forestry schools to earn master's degrees or doctorates.

Certification or Licensing

Voluntary certification is offered by SAF and requirements include having completed an accredited, professional level (bachelor's degree or higher) education program and having at least five years of professional forestry experience. Those who meet requirements receive the designation certified forester (CF) and must complete a certain amount of continuing education for certification renewal every three years.

Currently 16 states have some type of licensing or registration for foresters, and depending on state regulations, these may be voluntary or mandatory. SAF can provide some information on states' requirements. You should also check with your state to find out about specific statutes and regulations.

Other Requirements

Forestry requires above-average intelligence. Because of the nature of the work, the forester must often make decisions on the basis of incomplete knowledge. This means that you must be self-reliant and have a high degree of initiative. You should have an aptitude for science, curiosity, and a strong liking for the outdoors. Because trees grow slowly and the changes in forests are gradual, you must have above average patience and a firm conviction that the work you do is important. If you make mistakes or are careless, the results may not be apparent for many years. Therefore, you must be dependable and conscientious. While it is not necessary to have the physical attributes of athletes, you must have greater-than-average endurance and enjoy physical activity.

EXPLORING

One way to explore the field of forestry is to talk with someone already working as a forester or forestry technician. In some parts of the country, local chapters of the SAF invite prospective forestry students to some of their meetings and field trips. School guidance counselors may have literature and information on forestry careers. Also, colleges and universities that offer forestry degrees should have information packets for interested students.

If you live near forested areas you might be able to find summer or part-time jobs in forestry. Unskilled workers are sometimes used for certain tasks, and this type of work could be a good introduction to the field by providing valuable experience and offering a view of what the job of a forester is really like.

EMPLOYERS

Federal, state, and local governments are by far the largest employers of foresters. There are more than 29,000 foresters and conservation scientists working in the United States today. Of those, almost 40 percent of all salaried employees worked for the federal government, mostly in the United States Department of Agriculture's (USDA) Forest Service. Another 25 percent were employed by state governments, and 10 percent worked for local governments. While there are foresters' positions in every state, the majority of them are concentrated in the West and Southeast.

Foresters also work in private industry or are self-employed as consulting foresters. For those who work in private industry, employers include logging and lumber companies, sawmills, and research and testing facilities. Consulting foresters usually work with private or corporate owners of woodlands to help them manage their forests in the best way possible.

STARTING OUT

According to Ralph Unversaw, it is not easy to find a forester's position. "I was fairly lucky because there happened to be a job opening right when I applied," he says. "There just aren't that many foresters' jobs and the competition is tough."

Because the majority of foresters are employed by government agencies, forestry school graduates might first pursue this avenue of employment. Job seekers should check with their state and local governments for job listings, as well as with federal agencies, such as the Forest Service, Bureau of Land Management, National Park Service, and Bureau of Indian Affairs. Beginning foresters are often hired for government jobs on the basis of competitive civil service examinations.

Other foresters work for private industry, primarily for companies that manage forest lands for lumber, pulpwood, and other products. Newly graduated foresters should check with their college placement offices for information on job opportunities. Reference sections of local libraries may contain directories of wood products manufacturers, pulp and paper mills, timber firms, and conservation groups, all of which may employ foresters. Finally, the SAF maintains a list of resources for the forestry job seeker.

ADVANCEMENT

Professional foresters who have graduated from university-level schools of forestry often begin their first job with work that is not at a fully professional level. They may, for example, do the elementary surveying involved in forest inventory or engineering projects, work in logging or construction crews, or act as supervisors of planting or insect control crews. In progressive organizations, this training period is kept short and is meant to provide a real understanding of operations from the bottom up.

After such a training period, foresters usually move to more responsible positions. This almost always means an increase in office work and a corresponding decrease in the time spent in physical work in the field.

As foresters move on to positions of greater responsibility in a public or private forestry organization, they may be placed in a *line position*. A line position is one in which the forester supervises technicians and other foresters. At the lower levels, the forester in a line position might directly supervise two to five other foresters; at higher levels the forester may still oversee only a small number of people, but with each of them, in turn, being in charge of a small group of foresters. Success in a line position requires not only professional competence and knowledge but also leadership qualities.

Other foresters may move into research. In research work, the forester may begin as a laboratory assistant, work gradually into detailed research activities, and eventually move into leadership or administrative positions in forestry research. Some foresters who move into research choose to return to school for further education. With an advanced degree, such as a master's or doctorate, comes more opportunity for advancement, as well as better pay.

EARNINGS

According to the *Occupational Outlook Handbook,* median annual earnings of conservation scientists and foresters in 2000 were $43,640. Salaries ranged from less than $27,330 to more than $65,960.

In 2001, most bachelor's degree graduates entering the federal government as foresters, range managers, or soil conservationists started at $23,776 or $30,035, depending on academic records. Those with a master's degree start at $30,035 or $42,783 and those with doctorates could start at $52,162 or, in research positions, at $61,451. In 2001, foresters working for the federal government in nonsupervisory, supervisory, and managerial positions earned an average salary of $55,006.

Starting salaries for foresters in private industry are comparable to starting salaries in the federal government, but starting salaries in state and local governments are generally somewhat lower. Whether working for private industry or federal, state, or local governments, foresters' salaries depend on the number of years of education and their experience in the field. Workers in this industry usually receive a benefits package that includes health insurance, paid vacations, and sick leave.

WORK ENVIRONMENT

Foresters generally work a 40-hour week, although they must be prepared for overtime duty, particularly when emergency conditions arise. In the field, foresters encounter many different conditions, such as snow, rain, freezing cold, or extreme heat. They may sometimes be faced with hazardous conditions, such as forest fires.

The day-to-day duties of a forester in the field are often strenuous. "The job can be physically demanding," Ralph Unversaw says. "There's often a lot of walking."

Foresters whose work is more research centered may not find the physical requirements as demanding, since they may be spending more time in the laboratory. Their workweek also tends to be more regular and their routines somewhat less varied.

Most who choose a career in this field love nature and the outdoors; for them, a great benefit is being able to work in a beautiful, natural setting, free from the confines of a desk job in an office. "It's a great job if you like to be outdoors and walk through the woods," Unversaw says. "That's what I like best about it."

OUTLOOK

According to the U.S. Bureau of Labor Statistics, employment of foresters is expected to grow more slowly than the average for all occupations through 2010. Job prospects will be better for soil scientists and other conservationists than for foresters, however. Budgetary limitations have led to cutbacks in federal programs, where employment is concentrated. Also, federal land management agencies, such as the Forest Service, have given less attention to timber programs and focused more on wildlife, recreation, and sustaining ecosystems. However, a large number of foresters are expected to retire or leave the government for other reasons, resulting in some job openings through 2010.

There have been reductions in timber harvesting on public lands, most of which are located in the Northwest and California, also affecting job growth for private industry foresters. Opportunities will be better for foresters on privately owned land in the Southeast. Landowners will continue to need consulting foresters, as will private industries, such as paper companies, sawmills, and pulp wood mills.

FOR MORE INFORMATION

For information on forestry and forests in the United States, contact
American Forests
PO Box 2000
Washington, DC 20013
Tel: 202-955-4500
Email: info@amfor.org
http://www.americanforests.org

For information on forestry careers, schools, and certification, contact
Society of American Foresters
5400 Grosvenor Lane
Bethesda, MD 20814-2198
Tel: 301-897-8720
Email: safweb@safnet.org
http://www.safnet.org

For information about government careers in forestry as well as information on national forests across the country, contact
USDA Forest Service
PO Box 96090
Washington, DC 20090-6090

Tel: 202-205-8333
http://www.fs.fed.us

For information on forestry careers in Canada, contact
Canadian Forestry Association
185 Sommerset Street, Suite 203
Ottawa, ON K2P OJ2 Canada
Tel: 613-232-1815
Email: cfa@canadianforestry.com
http://www.canadianforestry.com/

Geologists

OVERVIEW

Geologists study all aspects of Earth, including its origin, history, composition, and structure. Along more practical lines, geologists may, through the use of theoretical knowledge and research data, locate groundwater, oil, minerals, and other natural resources. They play an increasingly important role in studying, preserving, and cleaning up the environment. They advise construction companies and government agencies on the suitability of locations being considered for buildings, highways, and other structures. They also prepare geological reports, maps, and diagrams. According to the U.S. Department of Labor, there are approximately 25,000 *geoscientists* employed in the United States, which includes geologists, *geophysicists*, and *oceanographers*.

HISTORY

Geology is a young science, first developed by early mining engineers. In the late 18th century, scientists such as A. G. Werner and James Hutton, a retired British physician, created a sensation with their differing theories on the origins of rocks. Through the study of fossils and the development of geological maps, others continued to examine the history of Earth in the 19th century.

From these beginnings, geology has made rapid advances, both in scope and knowledge. With the development of more intricate technology, geologists are able to study areas of Earth they were previously unable to reach. Seismographs, for example, measure energy waves resulting from Earth's move-

School Subjects
Earth science
Geography

Personal Skills
Helping/teaching
Technical/scientific

Work Environment
Indoors and outdoors
One location with some
 travel

Minimum Education Level
Bachelor's degree

Salary Range
$33,910 to $56,230 to
 $106,040+

Certification or Licensing
Voluntary (certification)
Required by certain states
 (licensing)

Outlook
About as fast as the average

DOT
024

GOE
02.01.01

NOC
2113

O*NET-SOC
19-2042.01

Two geologists examine the walls of a trench for evidence of ancient earthquakes. (Corbis)

ment in order to determine the location and intensity of earthquakes. Seismic prospecting involves bouncing sound waves off buried rock layers.

THE JOB

The geologist's work includes locating and obtaining physical data and material. This may necessitate the drilling of deep holes to obtain samples, the collection and examination of the materials found on or under Earth's surface, or the use of instruments to measure Earth's gravity and magnetic field. Some geologists may spend three to six months of each year in fieldwork. In laboratory work, geologists carry out studies based on field research. Sometimes working under controlled temperatures or pressures, geologists analyze the chemical and physical properties of geological specimens, such as rock, fossil remains, and soil. Once the data is analyzed and the studies are completed, geologists and *geological technicians* write reports based on their research.

A wide variety of laboratory instruments are used, including X-ray diffractometers, which determine the crystal structure of minerals, and petrographic microscopes for the study of rock and sediment samples.

Geologists working to protect the environment may design and monitor waste disposal sites, preserve water supplies, and reclaim contaminated land and water to comply with federal environmental regulations.

Geologists often specialize as one of the following:

Marine geologists study the oceans, including the seabed and subsurface features.

Paleontologists specialize in the study of rock formations, including remains of plant and animal life, in order to understand the evolution of Earth and estimate its age.

Geochronologists are geoscientists who use radioactive dating and other techniques to estimate the age of rock and other samples from an exploration site.

Petroleum geologists attempt to locate natural gas and oil deposits through exploratory testing and study of the data obtained. They recommend the acquisition of new properties and the retention or release of properties already owned by their companies. They also estimate oil reserves and assist petroleum engineers in determining exact production procedures.

Closely related to petroleum geologists are *economic geologists,* who search for new resources of minerals and fuels.

Engineering geologists are responsible for the application of geological knowledge to problems arising in the construction of roads, buildings, bridges, dams, and other structures.

Mineralogists are interested in the classification of minerals composing rocks and mineral deposits. To this end, they examine and analyze the physical and chemical properties of minerals and precious stones to develop data and theories on their origin, occurrence, and possible uses in industry and commerce.

Petrologists study the origin of igneous, metamorphic, and sedimentary rocks.

Stratigraphers study the distribution and relative arrangement of sedimentary rock layers. This enables them to understand evolutionary changes in fossils and plants, which leads to an understanding of successive changes in the distribution of land and sea.

Closely related to stratigraphers are *sedimentologists,* who determine processes and products involved in sedimentary rock formations.

Geohydrologists study the nature and distribution of water in the earth and are often involved in environmental impact studies.

Geomorphologists study the form of Earth's surface and the processes, such as erosion and glaciation, that bring about changes.

Glacial geologists study the physical properties and movement of ice sheets and glaciers.

The geologist is far from limited in a choice of work, but a basic knowledge of all sciences is essential in each of these specializations. An increasing number of scientists combine geology with detailed knowledge in another field. *Geochemists,* for example, are concerned with the chemical composition of, and the changes in, minerals and rocks, while *planetary geologists* apply their knowledge of geology to interpret surface conditions on the moon and planets.

REQUIREMENTS

High School

Because you will need a college degree in order to find work in this profession, you should take a college preparatory curriculum while in high school. Such a curriculum will include computer science, history, English, and geography classes. Science and math classes are also important to take, particularly Earth science, chemistry, and physics. Math classes should include algebra, trigonometry, and statistics.

Postsecondary Training

A bachelor's degree is the minimum requirement for entry into lower level geology jobs, but a master's degree is usually necessary for beginning positions in research, teaching, and exploration. A person with a strong background in physics, chemistry, mathematics, or computer science may also qualify for some geology jobs. For those wishing to make significant advancements in research and for teaching at the college level, a doctoral degree is required. Those interested in the geological profession should have an aptitude not only for geology but also for physics, chemistry, and mathematics.

A number of colleges, universities, and institutions of technology offer degrees in geology. Programs in geophysical technology, geophysical engineering, geophysical prospecting, and engineering geology also offer related training for beginning geologists.

Traditional geoscience courses emphasize classical geologic methods and concepts. Mineralogy, paleontology, stratigraphy, and structural geology are important courses for undergraduates. Students interested in environmental and regulatory fields should take courses in hydrology, hazardous waste management, environmental legislation, chemistry, fluid mechanics, and geologic logging.

In addition, students should take courses in related sciences, mathematics, English composition, and computer science. Students seeking graduate degrees in geology should concentrate on advanced courses in geology, placing major emphasis on their particular fields.

Certification or Licensing

Twenty-six states require geologists to be registered or licensed. Most of these states require applicants (who have earned a bachelor's degree in the geological sciences) to pass the Fundamentals of Geology exam, a standardized written exam developed by the Association of State Boards of Geology.

The American Institute of Professional Geologists (AIPG) grants the certified professional geologist (CPG) designation to geologists who have earned a bachelor's degree or higher in the geological sciences and have eight years of professional experience (applicants with a master's degree need only seven years of professional experience and those with a Ph.D., five years). Candidates must also undergo peer review by three professional geologists (two of whom must be CPGs) and pay an application fee.

The Institute also offers the registered member designation to geologists who are registered in various states and are not seeking AIPG certification. Applicants must have at least a bachelor's degree, be licensed by the state they wish to work in, undergo peer review, and pay an application fee.

Other Requirements

In addition to academic training and work experience, geologists who work in the field or in administration must have skills in business administration and in working with other people. Computer modeling, data processing, and effective oral and written communication skills are important, as is the ability to think independently and creatively. Physical stamina is needed for those involved in fieldwork.

EXPLORING

If this career sounds interesting, try to read as much as possible about geology and geologists. Your best chance for association with geologists and geological work is to join the clubs or organizations concerned with such things as rock collecting. Amateur geological groups and local museums also offer opportunities for you to gain exposure to the field of geology.

EMPLOYERS

The majority of geologists are employed in private industry. Some work for oil and gas extraction and mining companies, primarily in exploration. The rest work for business services, environmental and geotechnical consulting firms, or are self-employed as consultants to industry and government. The federal government employs geologists in the Department of the Interior (in the U.S. Geological Survey, the Bureau of Mines, or the Bureau of Reclamation) and in the Departments of Defense, Agriculture, and Commerce. Geologists also work for state agencies, nonprofit research organizations, and museums. Many geologists hold faculty positions at colleges and universities and most of these combine their teaching with research.

STARTING OUT

After completing sufficient educational requirements, preferably a master's degree or doctorate, the geologist may look for work in various areas, including private industry and government. For those who wish to teach at the college level, a doctorate is required. College graduates may also take government civil service examinations or possibly find work on state geological surveys, which are sometimes based on civil service competition.

Geologists often begin their careers in field exploration or as research assistants in laboratories. As they gain experience, they are given more difficult assignments and may be promoted to supervisory positions, such as project leader or program manager.

ADVANCEMENT

The geologist with a bachelor's degree has little chance of advancing to higher level positions. Continued formal training and work experience are necessary, especially as competition for these positions grows more intense. A doctorate is essential for most college or university teaching positions and is preferred for much research work.

EARNINGS

Graduates with a bachelor's degree in the geological sciences earned about $35,568 annually in 2001, according to the National Association of Colleges and Employers. Those with a master's degree averaged $41,100 and with a Ph.D., $57,500 a year.

The U.S. Department of Labor reports that the median annual salary for geologists, oceanographers, and geophysicists was $56,230 in 2000; the top 10 percent earned more than $106,040, while the lowest 10 percent earned less than $33,910 a year. In the federal government, the average salary for geologists in managerial, supervisory, and nonsupervisory positions was $70,763 a year in 2001.

Although the petroleum, mineral, and mining industries offer higher salaries, competition for these jobs is stiff and there is less job security than in other areas. In addition, college and university teachers can earn additional income through research, writing, and consulting. Salaries for foreign assignments may be significantly higher than those in the United States.

WORK ENVIRONMENT

Some geologists spend most of their time in a laboratory or office, working a regular 40-hour week in pleasant conditions; others divide their time between fieldwork and office or laboratory work. Those who work in the field often travel to remote sites by helicopter or four-wheel drive vehicle and cover large areas on foot. They may camp for extended periods of time in primitive conditions with the members of the geological team as their only companions. Exploration geologists often work overseas or in remote areas, and job relocation is not unusual. Geological oceanographers may spend considerable time at sea.

OUTLOOK

According to the *Occupational Outlook Handbook*, employment of geologists is expected to grow about as fast as the average for all occupations through 2010. In addition to the oil and gas industries, geologists will be able to find jobs in environmental protection and reclamation. Government agencies will have fewer jobs available because of cutbacks.

In response to the curtailed petroleum activity in the late 1980s and 1990s, the number of graduates in geology and geophysics, especially petroleum geology, dropped considerably in the last decade. Stability has now returned to the petroleum industry, increasing the need for qualified geoscientists. With improved technology and greater demand for energy resources, job opportunities are expected to be good, especially for those with a master's degree and those familiar with computer modeling and the global positioning system (GPS). Geologists who are able to speak a foreign language and who are willing to work overseas will also have strong employment prospects.

FOR MORE INFORMATION

For information on geoscience careers, contact
American Geological Institute
4220 King Street
Alexandria, VA 22302-1502
Tel: 703-379-2480
http://www.agiweb.org

For information on certification, contact
American Institute of Professional Geologists
8703 Yates Drive, Suite 200
Westminster, CO 80031-3681
Tel: 303-412-6205
Email: aipg@aipg.org
http://www.aipg.org

For information on student chapters, contact
Association of Engineering Geologists
PO Box 460518
Denver, CO 80246
303-757-2926
Email: membership@aegweb.org
http://www.aegweb.org

For information on the Fundamentals of Geology exam, contact
Association of State Boards of Geology
PO Box 11591
Columbia, SC 29211-1591
Tel: 803-799-1047
Email: asbog@asbog.org
http://www.asbog.org

For career information and job listings, contact
Geological Society of America
PO Box 9140
Boulder, CO 80301-9140
Tel: 888-443-4472
Email: member@geosociety.org
http://www.geosociety.org

Geophysicists

OVERVIEW

Geophysicists are concerned with matter and energy and how they interact. They study the physical properties and structure of the Earth, from its interior to its upper atmosphere, including land surfaces, subsurfaces, and bodies of water. There are approximately 25,000 geophysicists, geologists, and oceanographers employed in the United States, according to the U.S. Department of Labor.

HISTORY

Geophysics is an important field that combines the sciences of geology and physics. Geology is the study of the history and composition of the Earth as recorded by rock formations and fossils. Physics deals with all forms of energy, the properties of matter, and the relationship between energy and matter. The geophysicist is an "Earth physicist," one who works with the physical aspects of the Earth from its inner core to outer space.

This alliance between Earth and physical sciences is part of the progress that science has made in searching for new understandings of the world. Like the fields of biochemistry, biomathematics, space medicine, and nuclear physics, geophysics combines the knowledge of two disciplines. However, the importance of geophysics goes well beyond abstract theory. Geophysicists apply their knowledge to such practical problems as predicting earthquakes, locating raw materials and sources of power, and evaluating sites for power plants.

QUICK FACTS

School Subjects
Earth science
Physics

Personal Skills
Helping/teaching
Technical/scientific

Work Environment
Indoors and outdoors
One location with some travel

Minimum Education Level
Bachelor's degree

Salary Range
$33,910 to $56,230 to $106,040+

Certification or Licensing
None available

Outlook
About as fast as the average

DOT
024

GOE
02.01.01

NOC
2113

O*NET-SOC
19-2042.00, 19-2043.00

THE JOB

Geophysicists use the principles and techniques of geology, physics, chemistry, mathematics, and engineering to perform tests and conduct research on the surface, atmosphere, waters, and solid bodies of the Earth. They study seismic, gravitational, electrical, thermal, and magnetic phenomena to determine the structure and composition of the Earth, as well as the forces causing movement and warping of the surface.

Many geophysicists are involved in fieldwork, where they engage in exploration and prospecting. Others work in laboratories, where research activities are the center of attention. In general, their instruments are highly complex and designed to take very precise measurements. Most geophysicists specialize in one of the following areas.

Geodesists measure the shape and size of the Earth to determine fixed points, positions, and elevations on or near the Earth's surface. Using the gravimeter, they perform surveys to measure minute variations in the Earth's gravitational field. They also collect data that is useful in learning more about the weight, size, and mass of the Earth. Geodesists are active in tracking satellites orbiting in outer space.

Geomagneticians use the magnetometer to measure variations in the Earth's magnetic field from magnetic observatories and stations. They are also concerned with conditions affecting radio signals, solar phenomena, and many other aspects of space exploration. The data gathered can be most helpful in working with problems in radio and television transmission, telegraphy, navigation, mapping, and space exploration and space science.

Applied geophysicists use data gathered from the air and ground, as well as computers, to analyze the Earth's crust. They look for oil and mineral deposits and try to find sites for the safe disposal of hazardous wastes.

Exploration geophysicists, sometimes called *geophysical prospectors,* use seismic techniques to look for possible oil and gas deposits. They may use sonar equipment to send sound waves deep into the earth. The resulting echo helps them estimate if an oil deposit lies hidden in the area.

Hydrologists are concerned with the surface and underground waters in the land areas of the Earth. They map and chart the flow and the disposition of sediments, measure changes in water volume, and collect data on the form and intensity of precipitation, as well as on the disposition of water through evaporation and ground absorption. The information that the hydrologist collects is applied to problems in flood control, crop production, soil and water conservation, irrigation, and inland water projects. Some hydrologists study glaciers and their sedimentation.

Seismologists specialize in the study of earthquakes. With the aid of the seismograph and other instruments that record the location of earthquakes and the vibrations they cause, seismologists examine active fault lines and areas where earthquakes have occurred. They are often members of field teams whose purpose is to examine and evaluate possible building or construction sites. They also may explore for oil and minerals. In recent years, seismologists have contributed to the selection of missile launching sites.

Tectonophysicists study the structure of mountains and ocean basins, the properties of the Earth's crust, and the physical forces and processes that cause movements and changes in the structure of the Earth. A great deal of their work is research, and their findings are helpful in locating oil and mineral deposits.

Volcanologists study volcanoes, their location, and their activity. They are concerned with their origins and the phenomena of their processes.

Planetologists use data from artificial satellites and astronauts' equipment to study the makeup and atmosphere of the planets, the moon, and other bodies in our solar system. Recent advances in this field have greatly increased our knowledge of Jupiter, Saturn, and their satellites.

REQUIREMENTS

High School
A strong interest in the physical and Earth sciences is essential for this field. You should take basic courses in Earth science, physics, chemistry, and four years of mathematics. Advanced placement work in any of the mathematics and sciences is also helpful. Other recommended courses include mechanical drawing, shop, social studies, English, and computer science.

Postsecondary Training
A bachelor's degree in geophysics is required for most entry-level positions. Physics, mathematics, and chemistry majors can locate positions in geophysics, but some work in geology is highly desirable and often required, especially for certain government positions.

Graduate work at the master's or doctoral level is required for research, college teaching, and positions of a policy-making or policy-interpreting nature in private or government employment.

Many colleges and universities offer a bachelor's degree in geophysics, and a growing number of these institutions also award advanced degrees. An undergraduate major in geophysics is not usually required for entrance into a graduate program.

Other Requirements

If you seek employment in the federal government you will have to take a civil service examination and be able to meet other specified requirements.

You should also possess a strong aptitude in mathematics and science, particularly the physical and Earth sciences, and an interest in observing nature, performing experiments, and studying the physical environment. Because geophysicists frequently spend time outdoors, you should enjoy outdoor activities such as hiking and camping.

EXPLORING

You can explore various aspects of this field by taking Earth and physical science courses. Units of study dealing with electricity, rocks and minerals, metals and metallurgy, the universe and space, and weather and climate may offer you an opportunity for further learning about the field. Hobbies that deal with radio, electronics, and rock or map collecting also offer opportunities to learn about the basic principles involved in geophysics.

Some colleges and universities have a student chapter of the Society of Exploration Geophysicists that you can join. Employment as an aide or helper with a geophysical field party may be available during the summer months and provide you with the opportunity to study the physical environment and interact with geophysicists.

EMPLOYERS

Geophysicists are employed primarily by the petroleum industry, mining companies, exploration and consulting firms, and research institutions. A few geophysicists work as consultants, offering their services on a fee or contract basis. Many work for the federal government, mainly the Coast and Geodetic Survey, the U.S. Geological Survey, the Army Map Service, and the Naval Oceanographic Office. Other geophysicists pursue teaching careers.

STARTING OUT

Most college placement offices are prepared to help students locate positions in business, industry, and government agencies. Other job

Earthquake Statistics

Earthquakes occur on a daily basis, although most people aren't even aware of them. This is because earthquakes differ in magnitude, or the overall size of the earthquake. Using the Richter scale, seismologists give earthquakes a number that reflects the earthquake's magnitude.

The following table shows the annual averages of earthquakes of various magnitudes.

Descriptor	Magnitude	Average Annually
Great	8 and higher	1
Major	7–7.9	18
Strong	6–6.9	120
Moderate	5–5.9	800
Light	4–4.9	6,200 (estimated)
Minor	3–3.9	49,000 (estimated)
Very Minor	Less than 3	Magnitude 2–3: about 1,000 per day Magnitude 1–2: about 8,000 per day

Source: U.S. Geological Survey Earthquake Hazards Program (http://earth quake.usgs.gov)

contacts can be made through professors, friends, and relatives. Some companies visit college campuses in the spring of each year to interview candidates who are interested in positions as geophysicists. The college placement office can usually provide helpful information on job opportunities in the field of geophysics.

ADVANCEMENT

If employed by a private firm, a new employee with only a bachelor's degree will probably have an on-the-job training period. As a company trainee, the beginning geophysicist may be assigned to a number of different jobs. On a field party, the trainee will probably work with a *junior geophysicist*, which in many companies is the level of assignment received after the training has ended.

From a junior geophysicist, advancement is usually to intermediate geophysicist, and eventually to geophysicist. From this point, one can transfer to research positions or, if the geophysicist remains in fieldwork, to *party chief*.

The party chief coordinates the work of people in a crew, including trainees; junior, intermediate, and full geophysicists; surveyors; observers; drillers; shooters; and aides. Advancement with the company may eventually lead to supervisory and management positions.

Geophysicists can often transfer to other jobs in the fields of geology, physics, and engineering, depending on their qualifications and experience.

EARNINGS

The salaries of geophysicists are comparable to the earnings of those in other scientific professions. According to the U.S. Department of Labor, geoscientists (which include geologists, geophysicists, and oceanographers) earned an average annual salary of $56,230 in 2000. The lowest paid 10 percent earned less than $33,910 per year, while the highest paid 10 percent earned over $106,040 annually. In 2001, the average salary for a geophysicist working for the federal government was $79,660.

Both the federal government and private industry provide additional benefits, including vacations, retirement pensions, health and life insurance, and sick leave benefits.

Positions in colleges and universities offer annual salaries ranging from about $28,000 for instructors to $65,000 for full professors. Salaries depend upon experience, education, and professional rank. Faculty members may teach in summer school for additional compensation and also engage in writing, consulting, and research for government, industry, or business.

Additional compensation is awarded to geophysicists who are required to live outside the United States.

WORK ENVIRONMENT

Geophysicists employed in laboratories or offices generally work a regular 40-hour week under typical office conditions. Field geophysicists work under a variety of conditions and often the hours are irregular. They are outdoors much of the time in all kinds of weather. The work requires carrying small tools and equipment and occasionally some heavy lifting. The field geophysicist is often required to travel and work in isolated areas. Volcanologists, for example, may face dangerous conditions when visiting and gathering data near an erupting volcano.

OUTLOOK

According to the *Occupational Outlook Handbook*, employment of geophysicists is expected to grow about as fast as the average through 2010. The total number of graduates with degrees in the geophysical sciences is expected to remain small and insufficient to meet the moderate increase in industry job openings. This may eventually result in fewer employment possibilities in college teaching.

The petroleum industry, the largest employer of geophysicists, has increased its exploration activities, and more geophysicists will be needed to locate less-accessible fuel and mineral deposits and to do research on such problems as radioactivity, cosmic and solar radiation, and the use of geothermal energy to generate electricity. The petroleum industry is also expected to expand operations overseas, which may create new jobs for those who are willing to travel.

The federal government will need more geophysicists to study water conservation and flood control and to assist in space science projects. The growing need to find new sources of energy will undoubtedly make the work of geophysicists more important and more challenging in the next century.

FOR MORE INFORMATION

For information on geoscience careers, contact
American Geological Institute
4220 King Street
Alexandria, VA 22302-1502
Tel: 703-379-2480
Email: agi@agiweb.org
http://www.agiweb.org

For information on local meetings, publications, job opportunities, and science news, contact
American Geophysical Union
2000 Florida Avenue, NW
Washington, DC 20009-1277
Tel: 800-966-2481
Email: service@agu.org
http://www.agu.org

For information on student chapters at colleges and universities and services for elementary and high school students, contact

Society of Exploration Geophysicists
PO Box 702740
Tulsa, OK 74170-2740
Tel: 918-497-5500
Email: membership@seg.org
http://www.seg.org

Groundwater Professionals

OVERVIEW

Groundwater professionals are different types of scientists and engineers concerned with water supplies beneath the Earth's surface. For example, they search for new water sources and ensure safe water supply.

HISTORY

In addition to the water that can be seen on the surface of the Earth, such as lakes, streams, rivers, ponds, canals, and oceans, there is water under the ground, known as groundwater. Groundwater includes things like underground streams and aquifers, which are layers of water-bearing porous rock or sediment. People have been tapping into various groundwater sources for centuries, using the water for everything from drinking to irrigation.

Artesian wells, for example, are used to provide water (including drinking water) in some parts of the world. They are created by boring down into aquifers; the resulting pressure causes water in the aquifer to rise up in the well. Australia has the world's biggest artesian well system; in the United States, artesian systems supply water to parts of the Great Plains and the East Coast.

Like other natural resources, groundwater has been the focus of increasing attention in the United States since the 1970s. The U.S. government has recognized threats to this vital supply of water and passed laws to protect it. At first, people in the field and in related fields were called on to adapt their skills to meeting the new

QUICK FACTS

School Subjects
Earth science
Mathematics
Physics

Personal Skills
Communication/ideas
Technical/scientific

Work Environment
Indoors and outdoors
Primarily one location

Minimum Education Level
Bachelor's degree

Salary Range
$35,910 to $55,410 to
$85,260+

Certification or Licensing
Voluntary

Outlook
About as fast as the average

DOT
024

GOE
02.01.01

NOC
2212

O*NET-SOC
19-2043.00

regulations. In recent years, especially as the regulations have gotten more technical and complex, demand for people who specialize in groundwater science has risen dramatically.

A look at the groundwater situation in one state, Florida, demonstrates some of the potential problems. The groundwater in many areas is located not very far under the surface—just a few feet, in some cases. A surging population is drawing heavily on these supplies, threatening to use them faster than they can replenish themselves. Rapid development (farming, mining, construction, industry) offers high potential for disrupting the vulnerable groundwater.

Also, in some cases, below the aquifers in Florida that carry good water are aquifers that carry poor-quality water, high in sulfates. Drawing down too far into the aquifers that have good water might accidentally pull up the bad water from the aquifer below it, or, worse, pull over saltwater from the coast. Once saltwater gets in, that aquifer is probably lost as a source of drinking water.

Another groundwater hazard is the possibility of a fuel, chemical, or other spill on the ground. Hazardous chemicals in these substances can soak through the soil and reach the groundwater, contaminating it. Even good-quality groundwater usually is treated before it is used (although in some places, like outlying rural areas, people drink untreated groundwater, drawing it right out of the ground). Regular water treatment facilities are not designed to handle removal of hazardous substances. That requires special steps, is usually more difficult and expensive than cleaning surface water, and sometimes does not work.

This is, in fact, a national concern. Today, some 53 percent of the United States relies on groundwater for its drinking water. At the same time, better methods for detecting contaminants have revealed that contamination of groundwater is more extensive than was previously known.

Legislation (including the Resource Conservation and Recovery Act, the Comprehensive Environmental Response, Compensation, and Liability Act, the Superfund Amendments and Reauthorization Act, and the Safe Drinking Water Act) mandates the cleanup, monitoring, and protection of the nation's groundwater supplies. This direction was strengthened by later amendments to such laws. Recent stricter regulations applying to landfills, for example, acknowledge the potential risks of these operations to groundwater. In particular, seepage from landfills can get into the groundwater and contaminate it. New landfills must have double liners and other features to help prevent seepage; existing landfills have new

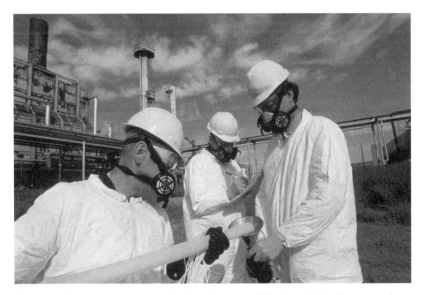

A team of groundwater professionals test sulfite levels in the ground-water near an industrial site. *(Corbis)*

rules about closing and capping the landfill to try to stop or mini-mize seepage. Groundwater monitoring equipment is used to take constant readings of the area's groundwater and determine if any seepage is occurring.

The special problems of groundwater, people's reliance on it, and the laws passed to protect it all have contributed to the growing need for groundwater professionals. No one really has the title ground-water professional; instead, it describes any of a number of different positions within the groundwater industry. These include different types of scientists, engineers, and technicians employed in govern-ment, private industry, and nonprofit organizations at various tasks designed to ensure safe, effective, and lawful use of groundwater supplies. In earlier times, geologists were often called upon to do groundwater work, and they continue to be important players in the field today. Geology is the science of the Earth's history, composition, and structure. Specialties in the groundwater field today include hydrogeology and hydrology. Hydrogeology is the science of ground-water supplies. Hydrology is the study of water and its properties, including how water is distributed and how it moves through land. Other professionals in the groundwater industry include chemists, geological engineers, water quality technicians, computer modelers, environmental engineers, chemists, bioremediation specialists, petro-leum geologists, and mining engineers.

Groundwater work is part of the water quality management segment of the environmental industry, which accounts for about one-quarter of all spending on the environment, according to the Environmental Careers Organization.

THE JOB

Employers of groundwater professionals include local water districts, government agencies, consulting firms, landfill operations, private industry, and others with a stake in successful groundwater management. What groundwater professionals do depends on the employer.

For example, local or regional authorities usually are responsible for ensuring a safe and adequate water supply for people in the area. Any time people want to make a new use of water or do something that might affect water in the area (like building a road, drilling a well, or laying a sewer), they have to get a permit. Before it will issue a permit, the authority has groundwater professionals check the site and decide if the use is safe. Typically, geologists do the necessary fieldwork, while engineers handle the actual obtaining of permits.

For a local or regional authority, groundwater professionals might help locate new sources of water in the area, which typically involves surveying the area, drilling for samples, and measuring the capacity of any water reserves found. They find the source of the groundwater and determine its ability to replenish itself if tapped for use, decide how the water would best be used, and make a recommendation to the authority. If the authority approves, a new well system is designed to tap the groundwater, and wells are drilled.

States are big employers of groundwater professionals. What groundwater professionals do for a state depends greatly on what part of the country it is in. The mapping of known groundwater supplies, often using computer modeling to show groundwater flow and possible effects of contamination, is often part of their efforts.

For both state and local or regional authorities, combating the effects of contamination is a critical task. The nature and extent of contamination, combined with the geologic and hydrologic characteristics of the surrounding land, determine whether the water supply is permanently tainted or can be made usable again in the future. Groundwater professionals design systems to reduce or stop contamination.

Consulting firms are also big employers of groundwater professionals. Regulations for waste treatment and disposal are becoming more and more strict, and that means that more technical expertise is required. Lacking that expertise themselves, many waste generators in the public and private sectors turn to consulting firms for help. Consultants may be called in to help with a hazardous waste cleanup around a landfill, at a Superfund site (an abandoned hazardous waste site), or at another cleanup, or they may help a private industrial company devise a system to handle its waste. Groundwater professionals can be very useful to such consulting firms. For example, if a landfill is leaking waste into a source of groundwater, a groundwater specialist could devise solutions, such as digging new drainage systems for the landfill or building new containment facilities. A groundwater professional with a consulting firm might work close to home or travel to job sites around the country or even around the world.

REQUIREMENTS

High School

At the high school level, you can prepare for a career in groundwater work by taking a lot of science and math. Technology is important in this field, so make sure you have computer skills. Also, focus on developing your writing and speech skills. Reports, proposals, memos, scientific papers, and other forms of written and verbal communication are likely to be part of your job as a groundwater professional.

Postsecondary Training

A bachelor's degree is the minimum requirement for being a professional in this field. According to the Environmental Careers Organization, geology, civil engineering, and chemistry are the most common undergraduate degrees in this field today. Other appropriate majors are engineering, geology, hydrogeology, geophysics, petroleum geology, mining engineering, and other related degrees. Another possibility is a degree in hydrology, although it is not currently offered by many schools. Appropriate course work at the undergraduate level includes chemistry, physics, calculus, groundwater geology, groundwater hydrology, engineering hydrology, and fluid mechanics. It is also a good idea to learn how to do computer modeling, mapping, and related tasks. Undergraduate degrees are sufficient for getting a job doing activities such as on-site sampling and measurement.

A degree in hydrogeology is usually obtained at the master's level. This degree and some experience will place you among the most sought-after workers in the environmental industry.

Certification or Licensing

Some certification programs have been developed to measure experience and knowledge of groundwater science. Both the American Institute of Hydrology and the Association of Ground Water Scientists and Engineers (a division of the National Groundwater Association) offer certification programs.

Other Requirements

Patience, persistence, curiosity, attention to detail, and good analytic skills are all useful for a groundwater professional. You would likely work as part of a team and have people to answer to, such as a supervisor, the government, a client, or all three. You would also probably have to be familiar with many regulations, often complex ones.

EXPLORING

You should hold one or more internships while in college (check with your college department for opportunities). You also might be able to find a part-time or summer job with a consulting firm. In addition, check into research opportunities with your professors at your school. You may be able to earn a small salary while gaining experience in fieldwork, compiling and interpreting data, or doing computer modeling. Volunteering for a nonprofit environmental organization might also be an option.

EMPLOYERS

Employers of groundwater professionals include local water districts, government agencies, consulting firms, landfill operations, private industry, and others with a stake in successful groundwater management.

STARTING OUT

There are many ways to find openings in the industry. One obvious place to start is the want ads, both in the daily newspaper and in various professional journals. Local chapters of groundwater and geological societies sometimes have lists of job opportunities or bulletin boards with important notices. New graduates can also look for work at state employment offices, local or regional water authorities, or the local branches of federal agencies.

ADVANCEMENT

Those starting out with undergraduate degrees are likely to do things like sampling and measuring work. Requisites for advancement will depend on the employer but probably will include some years of experience plus an advanced degree. It is advisable to keep up on the latest developments in the field through seminars, workshops, and other courses.

Advancement in private consulting firms will likely include promotion to an administrative position, which will mean spending more time in the office, dealing with clients, and directing the activities of other groundwater specialists and office staff. Those working for a local, regional, state, or federal organization may rise to an administrative level, meeting with planning commissions, public interest groups, legislative bodies, and industry groups.

Another option is for groundwater professionals to strike out on their own. With some experience, for example, ambitious professionals might start their own consulting firm.

EARNINGS

Groundwater professionals earn salaries in the upper range of those for all water industry professionals. The *Occupational Outlook Handbook* reports that median annual earnings of *hydrologists* (scientists who study underground and surface waters) was $55,410 in 2000. The lowest 10 percent earned less than $35,910, and the highest 10 percent earned $85,260 or more.

Benefits depend on the employer. They might include paid vacation, sick days, personal days, health and dental insurance, tuition reimbursement, retirement savings plans, and use of company vehicles.

WORK ENVIRONMENT

Fieldwork might mean going to natural areas to survey the geophysical characteristics of a site. Groundwater professionals may need to take water samples from the monitoring wells near a gas station, fuel storage facility, landfill, sewage treatment plant, or manufacturing company. They may oversee the digging of a new well system or check to see how a new well system is running. Although responsibilities depend on a professional's specific job, some work outside the office and outdoors is frequently part of the job.

In addition to fieldwork, groundwater professionals spend time working in offices. Some professionals, in fact, may spend most or all of their time indoors. Conditions in offices vary by employer, but offices are generally equipped with state-of-the-art technology. Most groundwater professionals work a 40-hour week, depending on project deadlines or unexpected developments in the field.

OUTLOOK

Like many environmental occupations, groundwater career opportunities surged in the 1980s in response to stricter government regulations. The field continued to grow through the mid-1990s but now is beginning to level off. Jim Lundy, a hydrogeologist employed by the Minnesota Pollution Control Agency, comments, "The field was burgeoning in the 1980s. I don't know whether we'll ever see growth like that again, but the field isn't going to contract severely either. As long as people continue to need water, there will be a need for groundwater professionals."

While this field may not be growing as rapidly today as it was 10 years ago, it remains a promising career choice for motivated, intelligent students. The continued growth of our nation's population makes finding and remediating groundwater supplies an even more pressing issue in the 21st century. Amendments to the Resource Conservation and Recovery Act, the Clean Water Act, and other legislation signal that groundwater is a priority to the government. Private industry needs to comply with stricter regulations, including those related to keeping groundwater safe from contamination. Local, regional, and state authorities need to map, develop, and protect their groundwater supplies. Consultants need the specific expertise that groundwater professionals can offer, for clients both in the United States and abroad. Research is needed to develop new ways to treat contaminated groundwater, to prevent spills or leaks, and to develop systems that will make the most of groundwater supplies. All of this means work for groundwater professionals for the near future.

FOR MORE INFORMATION

For the brochure Careers in the Geosciences *and listings of geoscience departments, contact or visit the following website:*
American Geological Institute
4220 King Street
Alexandria, VA 22302
Tel: 703-379-2480
Email: agi@agiweb.org
http://www.agiweb.org

The AGU's magazine Earth in Space *is designed for use by educators and science students. For details, contact*
American Geophysical Union (AGU)
2000 Florida Avenue, NW
Washington, DC 20009-1277
Tel: 800-966-2481
Email: service@agu.org
http://www.agu.org

For information on certification, student chapters, and related organizations, contact
American Institute of Hydrology
2499 Rice Street, Suite 135
St. Paul, MN 55113-3724
Tel: 651-484-8169
Email: aihydro@aol.com
http://www.aihydro.org

For information on grants, internships, and issues in geoscience, contact
Geological Society of America
PO Box 9140
Boulder, CO 80301-9140
Tel: 800-472-1988
http://www.geosociety.org

For information on certification, contact
National Ground Water Association
601 Dempsey Road
Westerville, OH 43081-8978
Tel: 800-551-7379
Email: ngwa@ngwa.org
http://www.ngwa.org

Hazardous Waste Management Specialists

QUICK FACTS

School Subjects
Biology
Chemistry

Personal Skills
Mechanical/manipulative
Technical/scientific

Work Environment
Indoors and outdoors
Primarily multiple locations

Minimum Education Level
Bachelor's degree

Salary Range
$19,406 to $28,517 to
$49,941+

Certification or Licensing
Required by certain states

Outlook
Faster than the average

DOT
168

GOE
11.10.03

NOC
2263

O*NET-SOC
13-1041.01

OVERVIEW

The title *hazardous waste management specialist* encompasses a group of people who do one or more of the following: identify hazardous waste, ensure safe handling and disposal, and work to reduce generation of hazardous waste. Because their duties vary so widely, hazardous waste management specialists may work for a number of different employers, from producers of hazardous waste such as industry, hospitals, and utilities to government agencies who monitor these producers. They may also work for the solid waste or public health departments of local governments. There are about 37,000 hazardous materials removal workers employed in the United States.

HISTORY

Today, hazardous waste management specialists oversee the handling of hundreds of substances the government identifies as hazardous to human health or the environment. However, this was not always the case. Prior to World War II, "hazardous waste" consisted of pesticides, which were under the regulation of the Food and Drug Administration, as well as by-products from a few industrial processes. Scientists and engineers who worked for the FDA or private industry monitored the disposal of these wastes to the minimal extent they were required to do so.

Before the environmental boom in the late 1960s, these wastes were handled much like regular garbage, dumped directly into open waterways, buried in landfills, and stored or buried in 55-gallon drums at the industrial site.

With the emergence of the nuclear age came a new waste that no one seemed to know how to handle: radioactive waste. This waste presented unique challenges because of its insidious nature; it is generally colorless, odorless, and remains hazardous for hundreds of years. Government scientists and engineers were the first to work on proper disposal with utilities that produced such waste (nuclear power plants). Today, hazardous waste management specialists work with these professionals on the handling of radioactive waste.

Postwar America also saw the beginnings of widespread use of synthetic materials: as one advertisement from the 1950s put it, America could enjoy "better living through chemistry." Unfortunately, this improvement also had a darker side: The tons of chemical wastes that chemical industries produced, in addition to some of the products themselves, were to have adverse and long-lasting effects on health and the environment that no one foresaw. Crude oil gushing from Union Oil Company's Platform A covered beaches in Santa Barbara in early 1969; only five months later the Cuyahoga River in Ohio caught fire. Public outrage directed at environmental disasters such as these signaled the end of such cavalier practices.

During the flurry of environmentally directed legislation in the 1970s, hazardous waste was not considered different from other types of pollution. The Resource Conservation and Recovery Act of 1976 gave the fledgling Environmental Protection Agency (EPA) power to assign permits for waste production and disposal, to track waste, to inspect facilities, and to fine offenders for noncompliance. That same year, the Toxic Substance Control Act forced manufacturers to submit formal notifications before they started commercially producing substances that could be toxic. Four criteria determine whether waste is hazardous: toxicity, ignitability, corrosivity, and reactivity.

This spate of legislation was thought to cover all aspects of hazardous substance management. But as the citizens of Love Canal found in 1978, this wasn't exactly the case. A rash of sickness there triggered an investigation that uncovered 21,900 tons of chemical wastes buried in 55-gallon drums that had leaked into basements of houses and the local public school. The resulting publicity led to the discovery of thousands of similar sites throughout the United States.

The Comprehensive Environmental Response, Compensation, and Liability Act of 1980 (CERCLA) was the political response to the furor surrounding these environmental crises.

CERCLA, or Superfund, as it came to be known, is a government fund that selects and pays for cleanup of abandoned, inoperative contaminated sites. Superfund also monitors new spills. Superfund established a National Priorities List of thousands of the worst sites, giving a budget and a timeline for completion of cleanup at these sites. In 1985, after a lukewarm beginning, Superfund was strengthened by the Superfund Amendments and Reauthorization Act (SARA). SARA expanded the environmental cleanup budget, allowed for civil suits against violators of the acts, and gave the EPA standards and deadlines to meet. Superfund undergoes constant review and evolution: Some companies hire individuals whose job consists solely of tracking Superfund and associated legislative changes.

Superfund is only one example of how opportunities have grown for people who specialize in the handling of hazardous waste. The evolution of environmental awareness has created jobs for people who can handle hazardous wastes that vary from monitoring leachate from municipal landfills to gases emitted from industrial smokestacks to chemicals buried years ago all over the United States.

THE JOB

Management of hazardous waste in the United States is handled in a variety of ways. Specialists may work anywhere along the continuum of hazardous waste management, preventing spills or contamination before they happen, helping to control them when they do, identifying contaminated sites that have existed for years, and cleaning up and disposing of hazardous waste.

Not all of the hazardous waste management specialist's time is spent in the field or in the lab. Because management of hazardous waste is highly regulated, there is a substantial amount of record-keeping and paperwork that hazardous waste management specialists are involved in. The cleanup of a contaminated site, for example, may take several months or even years. There is a bureaucratic process that must be followed. An example of steps a hazardous waste management specialist may be involved in before any cleanup proceeds includes: (1) identification of the hazardous substance and testing to gauge the extent of contamination; (2) search for or negotiation with parties responsible for the contamination; (3) writing of a plan of how best to clean up the site and how much it may cost; (4) waiting for several months or longer for approval and funding to clean up the site; and (5) public hearings to notify how, why, and when the cleanup will be done.

Because for many years hazardous waste was simply dumped anywhere, contaminated sites exist everywhere. Before hazardous waste laws such as SARA and Superfund were passed, for example, a paint manufacturer might have innocently dumped mounds of garbage containing toxic substances into a nearby field. Today, that dump may be leaking hazardous substances into the surrounding groundwater, which nearby communities use for drinking. Specialists study the site and determine what hazardous substances are involved, how bad the damage is, and what can be done to remove the waste and restore the site. They suggest strategies for the cleanup within legal, economic, and other constraints. Once the cleanup is underway, teams of specialists help ensure the waste is removed and the site properly restored. Some specialists supervise hazardous waste management technicians who do the sampling, monitoring, and testing at suspect sites.

Specialists who work for emergency response companies help stop or control accidental spills and leaks of hazardous waste, such as those that can occur when a tank truck containing gasoline is involved in an accident. Specialists working for hospitals or other producers of medical wastes help determine how to safely dispose of such wastes. Those working for research institutes or other small generators of radioactive materials advise employers about handling or storing materials.

Government-employed hazardous waste management specialists often perform general surveys of past and ongoing projects, assemble comparative cost analyses of different remedial procedures, and make recommendations for the regulation of new hazardous wastes. Government hazardous waste management specialists make detailed analyses of hazardous waste sites, known as Remedial Investigation and Feasibility Studies. Using data provided by technicians and other support personnel, these hazardous waste specialists weigh economic, environmental, legal, political, and social factors and devise a remediation (cleanup) plan that best suits a particular site. Some help develop hazardous waste management laws.

Other specialists work in pollution control and risk assessment for private companies. They help hazardous waste-producing firms limit their waste output, decrease the likelihood of emergency situations, maintain compliance with federal regulations, and even modify their processes to eliminate hazardous waste altogether. Hazardous waste management specialists might also help develop processes that utilize potential waste.

Common Contaminants

The following are some of the most common contaminants that must be removed from buildings and water and food supplies to ensure public safety:

- asbestos: heat-resistant mineral once used in building materials, but which was found to cause cancer and heart disease in humans

- copper: metal that can cause extensive damage to humans if ingested in large quantities, such as through drinking water

- lead: metal that was once used extensively in paint and fuels but which was found to cause developmental problems in young and unborn children

- zinc: although it is one of the most commonly used metals in the world, exposure to large amounts of zinc in soil or groundwater can cause harm to the body's immune system

- PCBs: human-made chemicals (often used in coolants) that have not been produced since 1977, when they were found to cause cancer and liver damage in humans

- TCE: a liquid used in many industrial solvents, TCE can cause a wide range of illnesses in humans; it is a major source of water contamination

Source: http://www.epa.gov

REQUIREMENTS
High School
High school students interested in preparing for careers as hazardous waste management specialists need to be strong in chemistry and other sciences such as biology and geology. English and other communications classes will help aspiring specialists in college and to effectively present their findings in their professional pursuits.

Postsecondary Training
Although some specialists enter this field with undergraduate degrees in engineering—environmental, chemical, or civil—it is not strictly necessary for the work involved. Many employers in this field train their employees with the help of technical institutes or community colleges with courses on hazardous waste disposal. A bachelor's degree in environmental resource management, chemistry, geology, or

ecology also may be acceptable. Areas of expertise such as hydrology or subsurface hydrology may require a master's or doctoral degree.

Certification or Licensing

Certification available to specialists is not universally recognized, and requirements for certification vary not only from state to state, but region to region, and year to year as well. After some years in the field, hazardous waste management professionals can gain certification through associations such as the National Environmental Health Association in Denver. Training for this certification can be obtained through job experience or course work provided by a number of institutes and community colleges nationwide. Some employers pay for workshops run in-house by these institutes to update their employees on such topics as emergency response, Superfund regulations, and emerging technologies.

Certification is also available through the Institute of Hazardous Materials Management. Although certification is not required, it lends weight to recommendations made by government-employed specialists and generally enhances a specialist's credibility.

Other Requirements

The relative newness of this field, its dependence on political support, the varied nature of its duties, and its changing regulations and technologies all require a large degree of flexibility from hazardous waste management specialists. The ability to take into consideration the many economic, environmental, legal, and social aspects of each project is key, as are thoroughness and patience in completing the necessary work. Prospective employers look for job candidates with excellent communications skills, no matter what their specialty, because this position is so reliant on the shared information of numerous professionals.

EXPLORING

Those who would like to explore avenues of hazardous waste management can get involved in local chapters of citizen watchdog groups and become familiar with nearby Superfund sites. What is being done at those sites? Who is responsible for the cleanup? What effect does the site have on its community? The Center for Health, Environment and Justice, founded by Love Canal resident Lois Marie Gibbs, may be able to provide information about current concerns of citizens (see listing at the end of this article). A book written by Gibbs, *Love Canal: My Story* (State University of New York Press, 1982) illustrates how the job of hazardous waste management specialist can make a difference in citizens' lives.

Additionally, understanding the problems of hazardous waste management and the controversy surrounding some of the limitations of Superfund provide a more detailed picture of the specialist's job. There are numerous magazines published on hazardous waste management, including those addressing the different waste generators and involved professionals, for example, chemical manufacturers, oil industry representatives, engineers, and conservationists. A few publications are *Integrated Waste Management, Journal of Environmental Quality* (http://jeq.scijournals.org), and *Journal of Natural Resources and Life Sciences Education* (http://www.jnrlse.org). Outreach programs sponsored by the Army Corps of Engineers offer presentations to high schools in some areas and may be arranged with the help of science departments and placement office staff members.

EMPLOYERS

Hazardous waste management specialists have opportunities with many types of employers. Federal, state, and local governments use hazardous waste management specialists in a variety of roles. On the local level, a hazardous waste management specialist may work in the public health, wastewater treatment, or municipal solid waste departments, enforcing local regulations and overseeing disposal of hazardous waste. Hazardous waste management specialists employed by the federal government generally have a regulatory role, overseeing the cleanup of past contamination and ensuring subsequent contaminations don't occur by monitoring those who generate waste. Hazardous waste professionals in government tend to have health and safety backgrounds. In the private sector, some specialists work for several companies as independent consultants. Still other specialists are employed by citizen groups and environmental organizations to provide technical knowledge about environmental and safety hazards that may not warrant Superfund attention but still concern citizens who may be affected by them.

STARTING OUT

Employers in this field prefer hazardous waste management applicants with hands-on experience. Volunteering is one good way to acquire this experience and gauge the field to find a suitable niche. Internships are available through the Environmental Careers

Organization (ECO), local nonprofit groups, and the EPA, among others. On-site experience at this level usually amounts to being a technician of sorts—running tests, preparing samples, and compiling data. Internships may pay minimal salaries, but most employers prefer candidates with even this kind of experience over applicants who have never seen how their education applies to real situations. Recent graduates and working professionals find jobs through trade association advertisements and on the Internet. Openings with government agencies can be found on the Web page of the Office of Personnel Management at http://www.usajobs.opm.gov.

Those who are still in school can start building a background now by attending public meetings in their area concerning hazardous waste. Read your local newspaper or call city hall or county government to find out what the local issues are. Citizen action groups that advocate environmental awareness are another good place to learn what the issues are in your area and perhaps volunteer your time.

ADVANCEMENT

To advance, hazardous waste management specialists need to be proficient in several aspects of hazardous waste management and able to handle an entire hazardous waste site or group of similar sites. This involves supervising other specialists, engineers, laboratory chemists, and various support personnel, as well as being the party responsible for reporting to regulatory agencies. Other specialists may find positions in public relations fields or higher management levels. Still others may seek further formal education and advance upon completion of higher degrees of specialization. The field of hazardous waste management is a diverse one, and after specialists have worked for awhile, the range of specialties available will become more evident.

EARNINGS

Hazardous waste management specialists who enter the field with no experience earn around $26,000 per year; those who have experience as an intern or technician start at around $38,000, according to the *Princeton Review*. Some 75 percent of hazardous waste workers are employed by the private sector, with middle-range salaries averaging between $40,000 and $50,000 per year. Specialists with degrees in areas of high demand, such as toxicology or hydrology, can earn $80,000 or more, depending on seniority and certification levels.

Specialists who obtain entry-level jobs with the government generally enter under the civil service classifications of GS-5 and GS-7 levels. In 2002, starting pay under the government's General Schedule was $22,737 for GS-5 and $28,164 for GS-7. However, the government notes that most of these jobs actually pay 5–12 percent more on average when adjusted for geographic location.

The *Occupational Outlook Handbook* reports that median hourly earnings of hazardous materials removal workers were $13.71 in 2000. Wages ranged from less than $9.33 per hour (or $19,406 annually) to more than $24.01 per hour (or $49,941 annually) for full-time work.

Specialists in the public and private sectors also enjoy benefits such as full health plans, vacation time, and subsidized travel arrangements. Employer-paid training is a common benefit in this field, as regulations and technology is constantly evolving and employers want specialists who are up to date.

WORK ENVIRONMENT

The complexity of the regulations often makes remediation work painstakingly slow, but also provides a measure of job security. High-publicity sites may bring considerable political and social pressure to bear on those responsible for their cleanup, especially if work appears to be moving very slowly. Competition for lucrative contracts can be fierce, and considerable effort must be made by employer and employee alike to stay abreast of changing technologies and legislation in order to be at the cutting edge of the field. The job of a specialist may require on-site exposure to hazardous wastes, and protective clothing that can hamper work efforts is often necessary. On the other end of the spectrum, there is always paperwork waiting to be completed back at the office. However, individuals in this field report a sense of accomplishment, and satisfaction in the field is extremely high. For some, the new developments that are a major part of the job provide welcome change and challenges.

OUTLOOK

ECO calls hazardous waste management a "hot" environmental career and calls for individuals with specific technical skills who can also see the big picture. As with some other highly skilled environmental professions, hazardous waste management is currently suffering from a lack of qualified professionals. The sheer enormity of the hazardous waste problem, with over 40,000 known sites and more expected to be identified in the near future, ensures that there will be cleanup jobs available as long as funding is available. An environmental careers survey recorded in the *Engineering News Record* cautions, "Though there's still a lot of hazardous waste to clean up, it's anyone's guess as to when it will be done." The higher-than-average growth rate for hazardous waste management professionals is expected to continue for at least the next decade. The U.S. Department of Labor also predicts that employment of these workers will grow faster than the average through 2010.

ECO advises students to plan for changes in the field; whereas the current emphasis is on waste removal, neutralization, and disposal, future job markets will revolve around waste prevention. Keeping track of trends in the field while still in school will enable students to tailor their education to the anticipated needs of the future job market.

FOR MORE INFORMATION

The following is a national grassroots organization founded by Lois Marie Gibbs and other Love Canal activists that offers publications on environmental health and community organization:

Center for Health, Environment and Justice
PO Box 6806
Falls Church, VA 22040
Tel: 703-237-2249
Email: chej@chej.org
http://www.chej.org

For information on certification, contact

Institute of Hazardous Materials Management
11900 Parklawn Drive, Suite 450
Rockville, MD 20852
Tel: 301-984-8969
Email: ihmminfo@ihmm.org
http://www.ihmm.org

The following association provides certification for hazardous waste specialists:

National Environmental Health Association
720 South Colorado Boulevard, Suite 970-S
Denver, CO 80246
Tel: 303-756-9090
Email: staff@neha.org
http://www.neha.org

For information on hazardous waste management training and degree programs nationwide, contact

National Partnership for Environmental Technology in Education
6601 Owens Drive, Suite 235
Pleasanton, CA 94588
Tel: 510-225-0668
Email: natlpete@maine.rr.com
http://www.ateec.org/pete

The following is a branch of the military that employs engineering professionals in hazardous waste management projects such as Superfund remediation sites:

U.S. Army Corps of Engineers
441 G. Street, NW
Washington, DC 20314
Tel: 202-761-0008
http://www.usace.army.mil

Land Trust or Preserve Managers

OVERVIEW

Land trust or preserve managers are part of private and federal efforts to preserve land or water from development; subdivision; pollution; overly heavy recreational, grazing, agricultural, or other use; or other human action. The management tasks of land trusts or preserves vary widely. Some positions involve field work such as monitoring the site, inventorying species, or managing natural resources to specialized conservation and preservation work. Examples of the latter might include doing controlled burnings, re-creating lost or damaged ecosystems, and restoring native plants and animals. Other positions are more traditionally administrative, such as fund-raising and community relations workers, land-purchase and development managers, legal and paralegal workers, and stewardship staff who monitor properties with conservation easements, work with owners or conserved land, and manage land owned by the trust.

HISTORY

Efforts to conserve land and water go back more than 100 years in this country and have been driven by two key forces: the government and private citizens' or community groups. Alarm about diminishing wilderness areas in the West led to the establishment of the first national parks and preserves by our government in the late 19th century. Around that time, the government also set aside four Civil War battlefields as national battlefield parks, the first historic sites so acquired by the United States government.

The single most influential figure in early conservation efforts was Theodore Roosevelt, the 26th president of the United States. Roosevelt fell in love with the West as a young man, when ill health led him there to seek better air. He owned a ranch in the Dakota Territory and wrote many books about his experiences in the West.

When he became president in 1901, Roosevelt used the position to help preserve his beloved West. He and his administrators pushed conservation as part of an overall strategy for the responsible use of natural resources, including forests, pastures, fish, game, soil, and minerals. This both increased public awareness of and support for conservation and led to important early conservation legislation. Roosevelt's administration especially emphasized the preservation of forests, wildlife, park lands, wilderness areas, and watershed areas and carried out such work as the first inventory of natural resources in this country.

Theodore Roosevelt was, rightfully, very proud of the monumental accomplishments of his administration in conserving the natural resources of the nation. He wrote, "During the seven and one-half years closing on March 4, 1909 (the years of his administration), more was accomplished for the protection of wildlife in the United States than during all the previous years, excepting only the creation of Yellowstone National Park."

But government action is only part of this story. Individual citizens forming private nonprofit land trusts, plus national nonprofit land trust organizations, have saved countless acres of land and water as well. They, too, have their roots in the last century.

Back in 1891, the city of Boston was bursting at the seams. A thriving shipbuilding industry plus other commercial and industrial pursuits had helped that city boom in the 19th century. Boston also had seen an explosion in immigrant population, particularly Irish immigrants. The captains of the industry and their families poured money into the arts, helping Boston gain a reputation as the "Athens of America."

Some Bostonians, however, were troubled by the rapid development that swallowed up areas at the edges of the city. They were concerned that remaining wild areas were going to disappear and that many people living in the city were never going to have access to open lands and wild areas.

One group of citizens took action. They formed a group called the Trustees of Reservations, bought up some of the undeveloped land themselves, and opened the areas to the public for recreational use.

This was the first official land trust in the country, and it paved the way for a whole movement of private land trusts.

Individuals and large groups have started land trusts. They have worked to protect just a few acres of land up to hundreds of acres, depending on the part of the country and the trust's resources. Sometimes trusts just acquire the land or easements on it; but sometimes, and increasingly so in recent years, they also take steps to manage it environmentally.

Land trusts saw very strong growth in the mid- to late-1980s. Following a slight dip in the early 1990s due to the recession, they are going strong today. In 2000, there were 1,263 private nonprofit land trusts.

Sometimes land trusts work in cooperation with U.S. federal agencies for managing lands. This is true of The Nature Conservancy (TNC), for example, a very large national land trust organization specializing in rare wildlife and habitats. "A number of things of rarity on this planet occur on public land," explains Chuck Basset, vice president of human resources for TNC. "We can help manage it, give advice, and counsel on it."

Consulting firms specializing in land trust or preserve management also exist and may be called in to help with special areas like ecosystem restoration or forestry management. Finally, some private corporations, such as utility companies or timber companies, own and manage large parcels of land; their land management may include conservation and preservation of areas such as forest wetlands.

THE JOB

Land trusts acquire land by buying it, getting the landowner to donate it, arranging for easements on it, or purchasing the development rights to it. Land acquisition may be just one of many tasks of a land trust employee, such as the executive director; or, in larger land trusts, it may be the sole job of one or more land acquisition professionals.

What is involved with managing a land trust or preserve? That depends on the specific land or water involved and its needs, who's doing the managing, how much funding and staffing is available, and other factors.

Staffing of land trusts can be minimal, particularly in the early years of the trust. At first, one person might do everything from handling correspondence to walking the land. If the land trust grows larger, it may add more people who can then focus on specific tasks, including management of the land. A few land trusts, particularly some of the large statewide land trusts, are large enough to have a staff of 30 paid people or more.

As for federally managed lands, these, too, can have varying levels of staffing and funding that affect what specific work is done. But the federal government employs about 75 percent of all people working in land and water conservation, and in general the federal agencies have greater resources than private land trusts. For example, all national parks have natural resource management departments that carry out tasks from ensuring environmental compliance to specialized conservation/preservation work.

Specific work varies in different parts of the country, from forests to the Everglades to coastal areas, and ranges from simple monitoring of the land to doing specialized work like recreating destroyed ecosystems. Examples include:

Planning for better use of land and water. If the land is a recreational area, for example, managers might plan how to prevent overuse.

Species inventory. Cataloging plant and animal species helps establish the "baseline" needed to plan for the area, explains Chuck Basset of TNC. "Our business is biodiversity conservation," he says. "So when we acquire land, we want to check the diversity there—species diversity, health of species, age of species. We hire contract or seasonal workers to do this; then stewardship scientists set up the plan."

Restoration or recreation of damaged or destroyed ecosystems. Getting an area back to how it used to be may involve cleaning up pollution, bringing back native species, and getting rid of non-native species. Landscape architects, biologists, botanists, ecologists, and others may help do such work. Restoration of wetlands, including forest wetlands, is one example of this work and may involve wetlands ecologists, fish and wildlife scientists, and botanists.

Habitat protection. Protecting wildlife habitats, particularly those of rare or endangered species, is another important task. At least 600 plants and animals in the United States alone currently are endangered, according to the U.S. Fish and Wildlife Service.

Prescribed burnings. Management of prairies, forests, or rangelands may involve controlled burnings. After the fire, specialists may go in and inventory species. Pitch pine communities in New York and New Jersey, and long-leaf pine forests in Virginia, Texas, and other parts of the South, are just some areas handled this way, according to Basset.

Rangeland management. In addition to prescribed burnings, this may involve controlled grazing by bison or cattle to keep plant life under control.

REQUIREMENTS

High School
Recommended high school course work for those interested in scientific work includes biology, chemistry, and physics as well as botany and ecology. All potential land trust or preserve managers can benefit from courses in business, computer science, English, and speech.

Postsecondary Training
At the undergraduate level, you might get a natural science degree, such as zoology, biology, or botany. There has also been growing interest in degrees in conservation biology, which focuses on the conservation of specific plant and animal communities, from schools such as the University of Wisconsin-Madison (http://www.wisc.edu). Another key program is the School of Forestry and Environmental Studies (http://www.yale.edu/forestry/admissions/index.html) at Yale University. Land and water conservation is a popular field, so if you are interested in the natural science areas, you are advised to earn at least a master's degree. One relevant program is The University of Wisconsin, Madison, interdisciplinary graduate program in land resources.

Other Requirements
Because land trusts tend to be entrepreneurial, they need people skilled in business administration, finance, and law to run the financial end of the trust, raise funds, negotiate deals, and handle tax matters. Communications professionals are needed to publicize the trust's work to raise funds.

EXPLORING

There are many ways to explore a career in land and water conservation. Read up on land and water conservation in the library, contact nonprofit land trusts or federal agencies for information about current projects, or check out the degree programs at local universities. The Internet is another rich source of up-to-date information; some sites are listed at the end of this article.

EMPLOYERS

The federal government, in its various agencies and branches, is the largest employer of land trust professionals. State and local government agencies also employ some land trust professionals in a variety of positions. Outside of government, potential employers include numerous nonprofit organizations and private land trusts. Additionally, large banks and other similar institutions employ land trust specialists.

STARTING OUT

This field is so popular that many people get their start in less traditional ways, such as contract or seasonal work, volunteer work, and internships.

Even people graduating with a master's degree may only be able to land contract work at first, according to the Environmental Careers Organization (ECO). Contract work is work done on a per-project or freelance basis: You sign on for one specific project and move on when it's done. Contract workers usually are specialists, such as ecologists or botanists, according to Chuck Basset. The need for them is high in the summer months, when biological inventory work is plentiful.

Volunteer and internship opportunities are available at many environmental organizations. These opportunities frequently lead to paid positions and always provide valuable experience.

ADVANCEMENT

There are three general advancement paths for land trust professionals. The traditional promotion path might begin with an internship, then progressing to positions of increasing power and responsibility. The second path involves expansion of duties within a specialty field. For example, someone who starts out as a land protection specialist in North Carolina may not have any desire to move out of that work; therefore, his or her job may be expanded laterally—broadening into consulting work in the specialty in other parts of the state, or even nationwide. Third, a person may opt for a "demotion"—getting back to land protection and conservation fieldwork, for example, after having served in an administrative position.

EARNINGS

The salary range for conservation professionals is about $20,600 to $25,500 for entry-level jobs, to an average of $42,750 and from $50,000 to $75,300 for people with a master's degree and experience.

According to the National Association of Colleges and Employers, graduates with a bachelor's degree in natural resources receive average starting salary offers of $26,000.

Federal government agency jobs pay more than state or local government jobs. Nonprofit groups' salaries can be competitive but tend to be at the lower end of the pay range. Salaries also tend to vary by region.

WORK ENVIRONMENT

The work environments for this type of career are as varied as the nature of the positions. Tramping around in the wilderness, inventorying plant and animal species, working outdoors to help develop a natural area—all of these are possibilities for people working in land or water conservation, particularly if they're working as a natural scientist or in support of the scientists. Many other land trust or preserver workers, such as administrators, communicators, lawyers, and fund-raising staff, will more often work in offices, of course, especially when they're working for larger organizations. ECO says people in land and water conservation tend to stay in their jobs longer than people in other environmental careers, attesting to the appeal of these jobs.

OUTLOOK

Right now, the best opportunities appear to be with the private land trusts and national land trust organizations, as opposed to the federal agencies. With little exception, none of the federal agencies is expected to see big growth over the next few years. On the other hand, following the slight slowdowns of the early and late 1990s, the private land trusts are growing.

Land trusts are the fastest growing arm of the conservation movement today, with approximately 1,263 in existence in 2000, according to the Land Trust Alliance (LTA). LTA's National Land Trust Census reports that local and regional land trusts protected 6.2 million acres as of December 31, 2000—226 percent more than they protected just a decade earlier.

FOR MORE INFORMATION

The following is a national organization of more than 1,200 land trusts nationwide:

Land Trust Alliance
1331 H Street NW, Suite 400

Washington, DC 20005-4734
Tel: 202-638-4725
Email: lta@lta.org
http://www.lta.org

This conservation organization offers fellowships for graduate work in conservation, places people in paid internships, and more.
National Wildlife Federation
11100 Wildlife Center Drive
Reston, VA 20190-5362
Tel: 703-438-6000
http://www.nwf.org

The following specializes in land trusts and land trust management for areas with rare or endangered species. Call 1-800-628-6860 for information about internships with TNC state chapters or at the TNC headquarters.
The Nature Conservancy (TNC)
4245 North Fairfax Drive, Suite 100
Arlington, VA 22203-1606
Tel: 800-628-6860
Email: comment@tnc.org
http://nature.org

SCA's monthly publication Earth Work *includes job listings. Also contact this group for information regarding volunteer positions in natural resource management, including with federal land management agencies.*
Student Conservation Association (SCA)
PO Box 550
689 River Road
Charlestown, NH 03603-0550
Tel: 603-543-1828
http://www.thesca.org

For information on land conservation careers, contact
The Trust for Public Land (TPL)
116 New Montgomery Street, Fourth Floor
San Francisco, CA 94105
Tel: 415-495-4014
http://www.tpl.org

INTERVIEW

Robert Linck is the regional co-director of the Vermont Land Trust in Montpelier, Vermont. He spoke with the editors of Careers in Focus: Environment *about his position and the field of land trust and preserve management.*

Q. Please describe the responsibilities of your job.

A. I co-direct the land conservation activities of the Vermont Land Trust's Champlain Valley Region and help manage the staff, operations, and budget for a six-person office. I assess the conservation values of land according to Land Trust criteria; negotiate or manage negotiations with landowners in conservation transactions; raise funds for conservation transactions from foundations, state and federal sources, communities, and individual donors; conduct outreach to landowners, communities, other nonprofit organizations, and the general public; represent the Vermont Land Trust before town boards, state agencies, the legislature, and the media; work with other staff on organizational policy and systems issues; and assist headquarters staff with annual and spring fund-raising appeals and membership events.

Q. What is a typical work day like for you? Do your responsibilities and/or interactions vary greatly?

A. Day-to-day work varies considerably, as suggested by the responsibilities described above. However, my primary focus is on the completion of specific conservation transactions, mostly involving land that is highly important to local communities for its productive farmland or forestland, recreational, wildlife habitat, ecological, watershed, or scenic values. Therefore, a typical day would involve phone calls, email, letters, proposal drafting, meetings, and staff discussions that help us complete conservation projects. Each project results in the donation or purchase of development rights and conservation restrictions, known more commonly as a "conservation easement," which is a legal document that is recorded in the land records and is binding on all future owners of the subject property.

The vast percentage of my time is dedicated to office work, ranging from informing landowners about conservation easements, learning about (and, when possible, accommodating) other landowner goals, researching conservation attributes of specific parcels, communicating with funders and conservation partners, arranging for the preparation of property maps, helping draft conservation easements, and attending meetings on current or potential conservation projects.

Q. What is your work environment like? Does your job involve travel?

A. I work in a very positive and relatively fast-paced environment, with dedicated co-workers, in a very well run nonprofit organization. Our office is in a small town, in a rural Vermont setting, and I do quite a lot of traveling around our region. Only rarely am I required to be away overnight.

Q. What sort of expectations did you have as you entered this field? Would you say the realities are much different?

A. I suppose I had fairly clear expectations when I entered land conservation work, in part because one of my college professors was associated with a local land trust. My first job involved a broad range of responsibilities, including land conservation, so I immediately immersed myself in the kind of work that I have come back to years later. Perhaps one misconception was laid to rest early on—most land trust employees do not spend vast amounts of their time outdoors. The other thing to note is that, perhaps like most jobs, much of what you learn happens on the job.

I should add that I've worked in many other fields within the broader category of environmental conservation (including water resources, advocacy, solid waste, research and education), and I have found land conservation to be the most satisfying— probably because successes can be so clearly observed.

Q. What course of undergraduate and graduate study did you pursue? Did this prepare you for your career? Also, did you complete any internships or special training for this career?

A. I have a B.S. in environmental studies and biology and an M.S. in water resources management. For five years in between those degrees I was employed by a nonprofit watershed organization. I participated in four internships during college, but none of those was oriented towards land conservation. Otherwise, the training for my current position has resulted from previous job experience and from workshops, seminars, and annual conferences of land conservation professionals organized by the Land

Trust Alliance. The Vermont Land Trust also conducts very effective staff training, as needed.

My educational background was very instrumental in my career, but the experiences of and relationships built through several internships and previous jobs were equally important.

Q. What other types of positions have you held?

A. I was regional (Vermont/New Hampshire) director for a four-state watershed organization—the Connecticut River Watershed Council; conservation director for the Adirondack Mountain Club; recycling coordinator for Warren County, N.Y. ; an adjunct professor of environmental studies at Adirondack Community College; an extension specialist for the Hudson River Estuary, New York Sea Grant/Cornell University; associate director for the Upper Valley Land Trust, Hanover, N.H.; and executive director of the Southeast Arizona Land Trust.

Q. How did you find your current job? What are ways one could look for work in your field?

A. The position was advertised in the local paper. I had a lot of connections to the conservation community in Vermont, so I was known to the Vermont Land Trust. The best way to learn about opportunities in the land trust community is through the Land Trust Alliance (LTA), which maintains a website that includes job listings. LTA also has a listserve that often has postings for position openings. The Nature Conservancy and the Trust for Public Land are national land trusts that also maintain websites with job listings. Direct contact with land conservation organizations in any particular region could also inform a job seeker of current or anticipated opportunities.

Q. What is the current outlook for growth and advancement in your field?

A. The outlook is very promising. Over 1,200 land trusts operate around the United States today. Though some of them are very small and may involve only volunteers, many more are already large organizations or are growing.

Q. What would you say are the most important skills and personal qualities for someone in your career?

A. You must be hard working and dedicated to the field of land conservation, loyal to the organization, have good "people skills," and the ability to speak and write clearly. You must also be efficient and able to juggle multiple responsibilities in a reasonably organized fashion and have knowledge of land conservation options and techniques, a willingness to participate in fund-raising, and a good sense of humor.

Q. What advice would you give to someone who is interested in pursuing a career in land trust or preserve management?

A. Fully understand the skill set required for the position you desire, take advantage of training opportunities, seek college/graduate-level education in existing or emerging programs that emphasize land conservation or a key skill associated with land conservation, and pursue opportunities to volunteer or intern at a land trust.

Many land trust jobs involve the type of work described above. Many other positions are focused on management and administration, geographic information systems (GIS) and mapping, fund-raising and community relations, or legal/paralegal work. For land trusts that own land and emphasize ownership and management of land or preserves, some positions will involve much more work outdoors, "in the field." Land trusts (including the Vermont Land Trust) that emphasize the stewardship of conservation easements have positions oriented toward landowner relations, "baseline documentation" of properties that have been conserved (GIS and mapping, field work with maps, GPS operation), field monitoring of private or public conserved land, interpretation of legal documents, and managing a legal process when conservation-easement violations occur.

Marine Biologists

OVERVIEW

Marine biologists study species of plants and animals living in saltwater, their interactions with one another, and how they influence and are influenced by environmental factors. Marine biology is a branch of science, and biologists in this area work in myriad industries, including government agencies, universities, aquaria, and fish hatcheries, to name a few. They generally work either in a laboratory setting or in the field, which in this case means being in or on the ocean or its margins.

HISTORY

Marine biologists started to make their study into a real science around the 19th century with a series of British expeditions. In 1872, the HMS *Challenger* set sail with scientists Sir Charles Wyville Thomson and Sir John Murray on the most important oceanographic mission of all time. Over four years, they traveled 69,000 miles and cataloged 4,717 new species of marine plants and animals. Many marine scientists view the reports from this expedition as the basis of modern oceanography.

Before this time, marine scientists believed that sea creatures inhabited only shallow waters. They believed that the intense cold, pressure, and darkness below about 1,800 feet could not support life. Then, in the late 1860s, the HMS *Lightning* and the HMS *Porcupine* made hauls from below 14,400 feet that contained bizarre new creatures.

Scientists began to build precision equipment for measuring oceanic conditions. Among these were thermometers that could gauge the temperature at any depth, containers that could be closed at a desired depth to collect seawater, and coring instruments used to sample bottom sediments. Scientists also figured out techniques for measuring levels of salt, oxygen, and nutrients right on board ship.

Twentieth-century innovations such as underwater cameras, oxygen tanks, submersible craft, and heavy-duty diving gear that can withstand extremes of cold and pressure have made it possible for biologists to observe sea creatures in their natural habitats.

THE JOB

Marine biologists study and work with sea creatures in their natural environment, the oceans of the world and tidal pools along shorelines, as well as in laboratories. These scientists are interested in knowing how the ocean's changing conditions, such as temperature and chemical pollutants, can affect the plants and animals that live there. For example, what happens when certain species become extinct or are no longer safe to be eaten? Marine biologists can begin to understand how the world's food supply is diminished and help come up with solutions that can change such problem situations.

The work of these scientists is also important for improving and controlling sport and commercial fishing. Through underwater exploration, marine biologists have discovered that the world's coral reefs are being damaged by humans. They have also charted the migration of whales and counted the decreasing numbers of certain species. They have observed dolphins being accidentally caught in tuna fishermen's nets. By writing reports and research papers about such discoveries, a marine biologist can inform others about problems that need attention and begin to make important changes that could help the world.

To study plants and animals, marine biologists spend some of their work time in the ocean wearing wetsuits to keep warm (because of the frigid temperature below the surface of the sea) and scuba gear to breathe underwater. They gather specimens with a slurp gun, which sucks fish into a specimen bag without injuring them. They must learn how to conduct their research without damaging the marine environment, which is delicate. Marine biologists must also face the threat to their own safety from dangerous fish and underwater conditions.

Marine biologists also study life in tidal pools along the shoreline. They might collect specimens at the same time of day for days at a time. They would keep samples from different pools separate and keep records of the pool's location and the types and measurements of the specimens taken. This ensures that the studies are as accurate as possible. After collecting specimens, they keep them in a portable aquarium tank on board ship. After returning to land, which may not be for weeks or months, marine biologists study specimens in a laboratory, often with other people working on the same study. They might, for example, check the amount of oxygen in a sea turtle's bloodstream to learn how the turtles can stay underwater for so long, or measure elements in the blood of an arctic fish to discover how it can survive frigid temperatures.

REQUIREMENTS

High School

If you are interested in this career, begin your preparations by taking plenty of high school science classes, such as biology, chemistry, and earth science. Also take math classes and computer science classes, both of which will give you skills that you will use in doing research. In addition, take English classes, which will also help you develop research skills as well as writing skills. And, because you will probably need to extend your education beyond the level of a bachelor's degree, consider taking a foreign language. Many graduate programs require their students to meet a foreign language requirement.

Postsecondary Training

In college, take basic science courses such as biology, botany, and chemistry. However, your class choices don't end there. For instance, in biology you might be required to choose from marine invertebrate biology, ecology, oceanography, genetics, animal physiology, plant physiology, and aquatic plant biology. You might also be required to choose several more specific classes from such choices as ichthyology, vertebrate structure, population biology, developmental biology, biology of microorganisms, evolution, and cell biology. Classes in other subjects will also be required, such as computer science, math (including algebra, trigonometry, calculus, analytical geometry, and statistics), and physics.

Although it is possible to get a job as a marine biologist with just a bachelor's degree, such jobs likely will be low-paying technician positions with little advancement opportunities. Most marine biologists have a master's or doctoral degree. The American Society of Limnology and Oceanography website has links to programs offering graduate degrees in aquatic science. (See the end of this article for contact information.) Students at the graduate level begin to develop an area of specialization, such as aquatic chemical ecology (the study of chemicals and their effect on aquatic environments) and bioinformatics (the use of computer science, math, and statistics to analyze genetic information). Master's degree programs generally take two to three years to complete. Programs leading to a Ph.D. typically take four to five years to complete.

Certification or Licensing
If you are going to be diving, organizations like the Professional Association of Diving Instructors provide basic certification. Training for scientific diving is more in-depth and requires passing an exam. It is also critical that divers learn cardiopulmonary resuscitation (CPR) and first aid. Also, if you'll be handling hazardous materials such as formaldehyde, strong acids, or radioactive nucleotides, you must be licensed.

Other Requirements
You should have an ability to ask questions and solve problems, observe small details carefully, do research, and analyze mathematical information. You should be inquisitive and must think for yourself. This is essential to the scientific method. You must use your creative ability and be inventive in order to design experiments; these are the scientist's means of asking questions of the natural world. Working in the field often requires some strength and physical endurance, particularly if you are scuba diving or if you are doing fieldwork in tidepools, which can involve hiking over miles of shore at low tide, keeping your footing on weedy rocks, and lifting and turning stones to find specimens.

EXPLORING

Explore this career and your interest in it by joining your high school's science club. If the club is involved in any type of projects or experiments, you will have the opportunity to begin learning to work with others on a team as well as develop your science and lab skills. If you are lucky enough to live in a city with an aquarium, be sure to get either paid or volunteer work there. This is an excellent way to learn about marine life and about the life of a marine biologist. Visit Sea Grant's marine careers website (http://www.marinecareers.net) for links to information on internships, volunteering, and other activities, such as sea camps.

You can begin diving training while you are in high school. Between the ages of 12 and 15 you can earn a Junior Open Water Diver certification, which allows you to dive in the company of a certified adult. When you turn 15 you can upgrade your certification to Open Water Diver.

Marine biologists examine a blacktip shark for a developmental study. *(Corbis)*

EMPLOYERS

Employers in this field range from pharmaceutical companies researching marine sources for medicines to federal agencies that regulate marine fisheries, such as the fisheries division of the National Oceanic and Atmospheric Administration. Aquariums hire marine biologists to collect and study specimens.

After acquiring many years of experience, marine biologists with Ph.D.'s may be eligible for faculty positions at a school like the Scripps Institute of Oceanography or the University of Washington.

Marine products companies that manufacture carrageenan and agar (extracted from algae and used as thickening agents in foods) hire biologists to design and carry out research.

Jobs in marine biology are based mostly in coastal areas, though some biologists work inland as university professors or perhaps as paleontologists who search for and study marine fossils.

STARTING OUT

With a bachelor's degree only, you may be able to get a job as a laboratory technician in a state or federal agency. Some aquaria will hire you straight out of college, but generally it's easier to get a paid position if you've worked as a volunteer at an aquarium. You'll need a more advanced degree to get into more technical positions such as consulting, writing for scientific journals, and conducting research.

Websites are good resources for employment information. The human resources section of an aquarium's home page will tell you whom to contact to find out about openings and may even provide job listings. Federal agencies may also have websites with human resource information.

Professors who know you as a student might be able to help you locate a position through their contacts in the professional world.

Another good way to make contacts is by attending conferences or seminars sponsored by aquatic science organizations such as the American Society of Limnology and Oceanography or the Mid-Atlantic Marine Education Association.

ADVANCEMENT

Lab technicians with four-year degrees may advance to become senior lab techs after years with the same lab. Generally, though, taking on greater responsibility or getting into more technical work means having more education. Those wanting to do research (in any setting) will need a graduate degree or at least to be working on one. To get an administrative position with a marine products company or a faculty position at a university, marine biologists need at least a master's degree, and those wanting to become senior scientists at a marine station or full professors must have a doctoral degree.

EARNINGS

Salaries vary quite a lot depending on factors such as the person's level of education, the type of work (research, teaching, etc.), the size, location, and type of employer (for example, large university, government agency, or private company), and the person's level of work experience. According to the National Association of Colleges and Employers' *Salary Survey* of 2001, those seeking their first job and holding bachelor's degrees in biological sciences had average salary offers of $29,235. The American Society of Limnology and Oceanography reports that those with bachelor's degrees may start out working for federal government agencies at the pay grades GS-5 to GS-7. In 2003 the yearly earnings at the GS-5 level ranged from $23,442 to $30,471, and yearly earnings at the GS-7 level ranged from $29,037 to $37,749. The U.S. Department of Labor, which places marine biologists in the broad category of biological scientists, reports the median annual income for all biological scientists was $49,239 in 2000. Income for marine biologists who hold full-time positions at colleges and universities will be similar to those of other full-time faculty. The American Association of University Professors' *Annual Report on the Economic Status of the Profession 2000-2001* found that professors (regardless of their subject area) averaged a yearly income of approximately $78,900. Those working as associate professors averaged $57,380, and those working as assistant professors averaged approximately $47,360 per year. Marine biologists who hold top-ranking positions and have much experience, such as senior research scientists, may make more than these amounts.

Benefits vary by employer but often include such extras as health insurance and retirement plans.

WORK ENVIRONMENT

Most marine biologists don't actually spend a lot of time diving. However, researchers might spend a couple of hours periodically breathing from a scuba tank below some waters, like Monterey Bay or the Gulf of Maine. They might gather samples from the deck of a large research vessel during a two-month expedition, or they might meet with several other research biologists.

In most marine biology work, some portion of time is spent in the lab, analyzing samples of seawater or collating data on a computer. Many hours are spent in solitude, reading papers in scientific journals or writing papers for publication.

Instructors or professors work in classrooms interacting with students and directing student lab work.

Those who work for an aquarium, as consultants for private corporations, or in universities work an average of 40–50 hours a week.

OUTLOOK

Generally speaking, there are more marine biologists than there are paying positions at present. Changes in the Earth's environment, such as global warming and increased levels of heavy metals in the global water cycle, will most likely prompt more research and result in slightly more jobs in different subfields.

Greater need for smart management of the world's fisheries, research by pharmaceutical companies into deriving medicines from marine organisms, and cultivation of marine food alternatives such as seaweeds and plankton are other factors that may increase the demand for marine biologists in the near future. Because of strong competition for jobs, however, the employment outlook should be about as fast as the average.

FOR MORE INFORMATION

The education and outreach section of AIBS's website has information on a number of careers in biology.

American Institute of Biological Sciences (AIBS)
1444 I Street, NW, Suite 200
Washington, DC 20005
Tel: 202-628-1500
E-mail: admin@aibs.org
http://www.aibs.org

Visit ASLO's website for information on careers and education. For information on membership and publications, contact

American Society of Limnology and Oceanography (ASLO)
5400 Bosque Boulevard, Suite 680
Waco, TX 76710
Tel: 800-929-2756
Email: business@aslo.org
http://www.aslo.org

For information on volunteer programs for in-state students and college internships, contact

National Aquarium in Baltimore
Conservation Education Department-Internships
Pier 3, 501 East Pratt Street
Baltimore, MD 21202
Tel: 410-576-3800
http://www.aqua.org

For information on diving instruction and certification, contact PADI.

Professional Association of Diving Instructors (PADI)
30151 Tomas Street
Rancho Santa Margarita, CA 92688-2125
Tel: 800-729-7234
http://www.padi.com

This center for research and education in global science currently runs more than 300 research programs and uses a fleet of four ships to conduct expeditions over the entire globe. For more information, contact

Scripps Institution of Oceanography
University of California, San Diego
8602 La Jolla Shores Drive
La Jolla, CA 92037

Email: siocomm@Scripps.ucsd.edu
http://www-sio.ucsd.edu

For reference lists, links to marine labs, summer intern and course opportunities, and links to career information, check out the following website:
Marine Biology Web
http://life.bio.sunysb.edu/marinebio/mbweb.html

For links to career information and sea programs, visit the following websites:
Careers in Oceanography, Marine Science and Marine Biology
http://scilib.ucsd.edu/sio/guide/career.html

Sea Grant's Marinecareers.net
http://www.marinecareers.net

Naturalists

QUICK FACTS

School Subjects
Biology
Earth science
English

Personal Skills
Communication/ideas
Technical/scientific

Work Environment
Primarily outdoors
One location with some
travel

Minimum Education Level
Bachelor's degree

Salary Range
$20,000 to $30,000 to
$75,000+

Certification or Licensing
None available

Outlook
About as fast as the average

DOT
049

GOE
11.07.03

NOC
2121

O*NET-SOC
19-1031.03

OVERVIEW

The primary role of *naturalists* is to educate the public about the environment and maintain the natural environment on land specifically dedicated to wilderness populations. Their primary responsibilities are preserving, restoring, maintaining, and protecting a natural habitat. Among the related responsibilities in these jobs are teaching, public speaking, writing, giving scientific and ecological demonstrations, and handling public relations and administrative tasks. Naturalists may work in a variety of environments, including private nature centers; local, state, and national parks and forests; wildlife museums; and independent nonprofit conservation and restoration associations. Some of the many job titles a naturalist might hold are wildlife manager, fish and game warden, fish and wildlife officer, land steward, wildlife biologist, and environmental interpreter. Natural resource managers, wildlife conservationists, and ecologists sometimes perform the work of naturalists.

HISTORY

The United States, especially during the 19th century, saw many of its great forests razed, huge tracts of land leveled for open-pit mining and quarrying, and increased disease with the rise of air pollution from the smokestacks of factories, home chimneys, and engine exhaust. Much of the land damage occurred at the same time as a dramatic depletion of wildlife, including elk, antelope, deer, bison, and other animals of the Great Plains. Some types of bear, cougar, and wolf became extinct, as did several kinds of birds, such as the passenger pigeon. In the latter half of the 19th century, the U.S. government set up a commission to develop scientific management of fisheries, established the first national park (Yellowstone National Park in Wyoming), and set aside the first forest reserves. The modern conservation movement grew out of these early steps.

States also established parks and forests for wilderness conservation. Parks and forests became places where people, especially urban dwellers, could acquaint themselves with the natural settings of their ancestors. Naturalists, employed by the government, institutions of higher education, and various private concerns, were involved not only in preserving and exploring the natural reserves but also in educating the public about the remaining wilderness.

Controversy over the proper role of U.S. parks and forests began soon after their creation (and continues to this day), as the value of these natural areas for logging, recreation, and other human activities conflicted with the ecological need for preservation. President Theodore Roosevelt, a strong supporter of the conservation movement, believed nevertheless in limited industrial projects, such as dams, within the wilderness areas. Despite the controversy, the system of national parks and forests expanded throughout the 20th century. Today, the Agriculture and Interior Departments, and, to a lesser extent, the Department of Defense, have conservation responsibilities for soil, forests, grasslands, water, wildlife, and federally owned land.

In the 1960s and early 1970s, the hazards posed by pollution to both humans and the environment highlighted the importance of nature preservation and public education. Federal agencies were established, such as the Environmental Protection Agency, the Council on Environmental Quality, and the National Oceanic and Atmospheric Administration. Crucial legislation was passed, including the Wilderness Act (1964) and the Endangered Species Act (1969). Naturalists have been closely involved with these conservation efforts and others, shouldering the responsibility to communicate to the public the importance of maintaining diverse ecosystems and to help restore or balance ecosystems under threat.

THE JOB

Because of the impact of human populations on the environment, virtually no area in the United States is truly wild. Land and the animal populations require human intervention to help battle against the human encroachment that is damaging or hindering wildlife. Naturalists work to help wildlife maintain or improve their hold in the world.

The work can be directly involved in maintaining individual populations of animals or plants, overseeing whole ecosystems, or promoting the work of those who are directly involved in the maintenance of the ecosystem. Fish and wildlife officers (or fish and game wardens) work to preserve and restore the animal populations, including migratory birds that may only be part of the environment temporarily. For more information on this career, see the article "Fish and Game Wardens." Wildlife managers and range conservationists oversee the combination of plants and animals in their territories.

Wildlife managers, range managers, and *conservationists* work to maintain the plant and animal life in a given area. Wildlife managers can work in small local parks or enormous national parks. Range managers work on ranges that have a combination of domestic livestock and wild population. The U.S. government has leased and permitted farmers to graze and raise livestock on federally held ranges, although this program is under increasing attack by conservationists. Range managers must ensure that both the domestic and wild populations are living side by side successfully. They make sure that the population of predatory wild animals does not increase enough to deplete the livestock and that the livestock does not overgraze the land and eliminate essential food for the wild animals. Range managers and conservationists must test soil and water for nutrients and pollution, count plant and animal populations in every season, and keep in contact with farmers using the land for reports of attacks on livestock or the presence of disease.

Wildlife managers also balance the needs of the humans using or traveling through the land they supervise and the animals that live in or travel through that same land. They keep track of the populations of animals and plants and provide food and water when it is lacking naturally. This may involve airdrops of hay and grain during winter months to deer, moose, or elk populations in remote reaches of a national forest, or digging and filling a water reservoir for animals during a drought.

Naturalists in all these positions often have administrative duties such as supervising staff members and volunteers, raising funds (particularly for independent nonprofit organizations), writing grant applications, taking and keeping records and statistics, and maintaining public relations. They may write articles for local or national publications to inform and educate the public about their location or a specific project. They may be interviewed by journalists for reports concerning their site or their work.

Nature walks are often given to groups as a way of educating people about the land and the work that goes into revitalizing and maintaining it. Tourists, schoolchildren, amateur conservationists and naturalists, social clubs, and retirees commonly attend these walks. On a nature walk, the naturalist may point out specific plants and animals, identify rocks, and discuss soil composition or the natural history of the area (including special environmental strengths and problems). The naturalist may even discuss the indigenous people of the area, especially in terms of how they adapted to the unique aspects of their particular environment. Because such a variety of topics may be brought up, the naturalist must be an environmental generalist, familiar with such subjects as biology, botany, geology, geography, meteorology, anthropology, and history.

Demonstrations, exhibits, and classes are ways that the naturalist can educate the public about the environment. For example, to help children understand oil spills, the naturalist may set up a simple demonstration showing that oil and water do not mix. Sometimes the natural setting already provides an exhibit for the naturalist. Dead fish, birds, and other animals found in a park may help demonstrate the natural life cycle and the process of decomposition. Instruction may also be given on outdoor activities, such as hiking and camping.

For some naturalists, preparing educational materials is a large part of their job. Brochures, fact sheets, pamphlets, and newsletters may be written for people visiting the park or nature center. Materials might also be sent to area residents in an effort to gain public support.

One aspect of protecting any natural area involves communicating facts and debunking myths about how to respect the area and the flora and fauna that inhabit it. Another aspect involves tending managed areas to promote a diversity of plants and animals. This may mean introducing trails and footpaths that provide easy yet noninvasive access for the public; it may mean cordoning off an area to prevent foot traffic from ruining a patch of rare moss; or it may mean instigating a letter-writing campaign to drum up support for legislation to protect a specific area, plant, or animal. It may be easy to get support for protecting the snowshoe rabbit; it is harder to make the public understand the need to preserve and maintain a bat cave.

Some naturalists, such as directors of nature centers or conservation organizations, have massive administrative responsibilities. They might recruit volunteers and supervise staff, organize long- and short-term program goals, and handle record-keeping and the budget. To raise money, naturalists may need to speak publicly on a regular basis, write grant proposals, and organize and attend scheduled fund-raising activities and community meetings. Naturalists also try to increase public awareness and support by writing press releases and organizing public workshops, conferences, seminars, meetings, and hearings. In general, naturalists must be available as resources for educating and advising the community.

REQUIREMENTS

High School
If you are interested in this field, you should take a number of basic science courses, including biology, chemistry, and Earth science. Botany courses and clubs are helpful, since they provide direct experience monitoring plant growth and health. Animal care experience, usually obtained through volunteer work, also is helpful. Take English courses in high school to improve your writing skills, which you will use when writing grant proposals and conducting research.

Postsecondary Training
An undergraduate degree in environmental, physical, or natural sciences is generally the minimum educational requirement for becoming a naturalist. Common college majors are biology, forestry, wildlife management, natural resource and park management, natural resources, botany, zoology, chemistry, natural history, and environmental science. Course work in economics, history, anthropology, English, international studies, and communication arts are also helpful.

Graduate education is increasingly required for employment as a naturalist, particularly for upper-level positions. A master's degree in natural science or natural resources is the minimum requirement for supervisory or administrative roles in many of the nonprofit agencies, and several positions require either a doctorate or several years of experience in the field. For positions in agencies with international sites, work abroad is necessary and can be obtained through volunteer positions such as those with the Peace Corps or in paid positions assisting in site administration and management.

Other Requirements
If you are considering a career in this field, you should like working outdoors, as most naturalists spend the majority of their time outside in all kinds of weather. However, along with the desire to work in and

with nature, you need to be capable of communicating with people as well. Excellent writing skills are helpful in preparing educational materials and grant proposals.

Seemingly unrelated skills in this field, such as engine repair and basic carpentry, can be essential to managing a post. Because of the remote locations of many of the work sites, self-sufficiency in operating and maintaining the equipment allows the staff to lose fewer days because of equipment breakdown.

EXPLORING

One of the best ways to learn about the job of a naturalist is to volunteer at one of the many national and state parks or nature centers. These institutions often recruit volunteers for outdoor work. College students, for example, are sometimes hired to work as summer or part-time nature guides. Outdoor recreation and training organizations, such as Outward Bound and the National Outdoor Leadership School, are especially good resources. Most volunteer positions, though, require a high school diploma and some college credit.

You should also consider college internship programs. In addition, conservation programs and organizations throughout the country and the world offer opportunities for volunteer work in a wide variety of areas, including working with the public, giving lectures and guided tours, and working with others to build or maintain an ecosystem. For more frequent, up-to-date information, you can subscribe to one of several newsletters that post internship and job positions. *Environmental Careers World* (http://environmental-jobs.com/index.htm) and *Environmental Career Opportunities* (http://eco-jobs.com) are two newsletters to look for.

EMPLOYERS

Naturalists may be employed by state agencies such as departments of wildlife, departments of fish and game, or departments of natural resources. They may work at the federal level for the U.S. Fish and Wildlife Service. Naturalists may also work in the private sector for such employers as nature centers, arboretums, and botanical gardens.

STARTING OUT

If you hope to become a park employee, the usual method of entry is through part-time or seasonal employment for the first several jobs, then a full-time position. Because it is difficult to get experience before completing a college degree, and because seasonal employment is common, you should prepare to seek supplemental income for your first few years in the field.

International experience is helpful with agencies that work beyond the U.S. borders. This can be through the Peace Corps or other volunteer organizations that work with local populations on land and habitat management or restoration. Other volunteer experience is available through local restoration programs on sites in your area. Organizations such as the Nature Conservancy (http://nature.org), Open Lands, and many others buy land to restore, and these organizations rely extensively on volunteer labor for stewarding and working the land. Rescue and release centers work with injured and abandoned wildlife to rehabilitate them. Opportunities at these centers can include banding wild animals for tracking, working with injured or adolescent animals for release training, and adapting unreleasable animals to educational programs and presentations.

ADVANCEMENT

In some settings, such as small nature centers, there may be little room for advancement. In larger organizations, experience and additional education can lead to increased responsibility and pay. Among the higher level positions is that of director, handling supervisory, administrative, and public relations tasks.

Advancement into upper-level management and supervisory positions usually requires a graduate degree, although people with a graduate degree and no work experience will still have to start in nearly entry-level positions. So you can either work a few years and then return to school to get an advanced degree or complete your education and start in the same position as you would have without the degree. The advanced degree will allow you eventually to move further up in the organizational structure.

EARNINGS

Earnings for naturalists are influenced by several factors, including the naturalist's specific job (for example, a wildlife biologist, a water and soil conservationist, or a game manager), the employer (for example, a state or federal agency), and the naturalist's experience and education. The U.S. Fish and Wildlife Service reports that biologists working for this department have starting salaries at the GS-5 to GS-7 levels. In 2003, biologists at the GS-5 pay level earned an annual

Charles Darwin, Naturalist

Charles Darwin (1809–1882) was a British naturalist who coined the theories of evolution and natural selection. He was born on February 12, 1809, in Shrewsbury, England. His father, Robert Darwin, was a physician, and his grandfather, Erasmus Darwin, was a philosopher and a naturalist. Charles's mother, Susannah Darwin, died when he was eight years old.

At the age of 16, Darwin entered Edinburgh University to study medicine. He eventually transferred to Cambridge University to prepare to become a clergyman in the Church of England.

When he was 22, Darwin served as an unpaid naturalist aboard the HMS *Beagle,* which was a British science expedition to the Pacific coast of South America. He studied plants and animals and was especially intrigued by his findings in the Galapagos Islands of fossils that were similar to modern species. Upon his return from the five-year voyage, Darwin studied his notes and developed several theories, including those on evolutionary change, specialization, and natural selection.

In 1859, Darwin published *The Origin of Species,* one of his most famous and controversial books. Darwin lived with his wife and children outside of London until he died on April 19, 1882. He is buried in Westminster Abbey. Darwin's theories remain controversial and have had a great impact on religious and scientific thought.

salary of $23,442, and those at the GS-7 level earned $29,037. The U.S. Fish and Wildlife Service further reports that biologists can expect to advance to GS-11 or GS-12 levels. In 2003, basic yearly pay at these levels was $42,976 and $51,508, respectively. In general, those working for state agencies have somewhat lower earnings, particularly at the entry level. And, again, the specific job a naturalist performs affects earnings. For example, the U.S. Department of Labor's *2001 National Occupational Employment and Wage Estimates* reports that conservation scientists had a median annual salary of $48,970. However, some conservation workers put in 40-hour weeks and make less than $20,000 annually. As with other fields, management positions are among the highest paying. For example, in 2002, the Idaho Department of Fish and Game advertised an opening for a wildlife game manager, offering a pay range of $22.78–$35.59 per hour. These hourly wages translate into approximately $47,380–$74,025 per year for full-time work. Keep in mind, though, that this position and these earnings are at the top of the field. The candidate who meets the qualifications for this position would have extensive experience and be responsible for, among other things, managing research pro-grams statewide, hiring lower level managers, prioritizing and direct-ing research, and acting as the department representative to other government agencies and public groups.

For some positions, housing and vehicles may be provided. Other benefits, depending on employer, may include health insurance, vaca-tion time, and retirement plans.

WORK ENVIRONMENT

Field naturalists spend a majority of their working hours outdoors. Depending on the location, the naturalist must work in a wide variety of weather conditions: from frigid cold to sweltering heat to torrential rain. Remote sites are common, and long periods of working either in isolation or in small teams is not uncommon for field research and management. Heavy lifting, hauling, working with machinery and hand tools, digging, planting, harvesting, and tracking may fall to the naturalist working in the field. One wildlife manager in Montana spent every daylight hour for several days in a row literally running up and down snow-covered mountains, attempting to tranquilize and collar a mountain lion. Clearly, this can be a physically demanding job.

Indoor work includes scheduling, planning, and classroom teach-ing. Data gathering and maintaining logs and records are required for many jobs. Naturalists may need to attend and speak at local com-munity meetings. They may have to read detailed legislative bills to analyze the impact of legislation before it becomes law.

Those in supervisory positions, such as directors, are often so busy with administrative and organizational tasks that they may spend lit-tle of their workday outdoors. Work that includes guided tours and walks through nature areas is frequently seasonal and usually depend-ent on daily visitors.

Full-time naturalists usually work about 35–40 hours per week. Overtime is often required, and for those naturalists working in areas visited by campers, camping season is extremely busy and can require much overtime. Wildlife and range managers may be on call during storms and severe weather. Seasonal work, such as burn season for land managers and stewards, may require overtime and frequent weekend work.

Naturalists have special occupational hazards, such as working with helicopters, small airplanes, all-terrain vehicles, and other modes of transport through rugged landscapes and into remote regions. Adverse weather conditions and working in rough terrain make illness and injury more likely. Naturalists must be able to get along with the variety of people using the area and may encounter armed individuals who are poaching or otherwise violating the law.

Naturalists also have a number of unique benefits. Most prominent is the chance to live and work in some of the most beautiful places in the world. For many individuals, the lower salaries are offset by the recreational and lifestyle opportunities afforded by living and working in such scenic areas. In general, occupational stress is low, and most naturalists appreciate the opportunity to continually learn about and work to improve the environment.

OUTLOOK

The outlook for naturalists is expected to be fair in the first decade of the 21st century. While a growing public concern about environmental issues may cause an increased demand for naturalists, this trend could be offset by government cutbacks in funding for nature programs. Reduced government spending on education may indirectly affect the demand for naturalists, as school districts would have less money to spend on outdoor education and recreation. Despite the limited number of available positions, the number of well-qualified applicants is expected to remain high.

FOR MORE INFORMATION

For information on environmental expeditions, contact
Earthwatch Institute
3 Clock Tower Place, Suite 100
PO Box 75
Maynard, MA 01754
Tel: 800-776-0188
Email: info@earthwatch.org
http://www.earthwatch.org

For information about internships, career conferences, and publications, such as the Environmental Career Resources Guide, *contact*
Environmental Careers Organization
179 South Street
Boston, MA 02111
Tel: 617-426-4375
http://www.eco.org

This group offers internships and fellowships for college and graduate students with an interest in environmental issues. For information, contact

Friends of the Earth
1717 Massachusetts Avenue, NW, Suite 600
Washington, DC 20036
Tel: 877-843-8687
Email: foe@foe.org
http://www.foe.org

For information on environmental issues, services, events, news, and job listings, check out the following websites

Institute for Global Communications
PO Box 29904
San Francisco, CA 94129-0904
Email: support@igc.apc.org
http://www.igc.org/home/econet/index.html

National Wildlife Federation
11100 Wildlife Center Drive
Reston, VA 20190-5362
Tel: 800-822-9919
http://www.nwf.org

Oceanographers

OVERVIEW

Oceanographers obtain information about the ocean through observations, surveys, and experiments. They study the physical, chemical, and biological composition of the ocean and the geological structure of the seabed. They also analyze phenomena involving the water itself, the atmosphere above it, the land beneath it, and the coastal borders. They study acoustical properties of water so that a comprehensive and unified picture of the ocean's behavior may be developed. A *limnologist* is a specialist who studies freshwater life.

HISTORY

The oceans hold approximately 97 percent of the water on Earth and cover more than two-thirds of its surface. Oceans hold food, chemicals, and minerals, yet oceanography is a fairly new science. In fact, according to the Oceanography Society, it was only during the 20th century that we got the first global glimpse of how the oceans work. With such inventions as deep-sea diving gear, scuba, and the bathysphere (a steel diving sphere for deep-sea observation), scientists are undertaking more detailed studies of underwater life. Oceanography includes studying air and sea interaction in weather forecasting, solving sea mining problems, predicting and preventing pollution, studying sea life, and improving methods of deriving foods from the ocean.

THE JOB

Oceanographers collect and study data about the motions of ocean water (waves, currents, and tides), marine life (sea plants and animals), ore and petroleum deposits (minerals and oils contained in the nodules and oozes of the ocean floor), and the contour of the ocean floor (ocean mountains, valleys, and depths). Many of their findings are compiled for maps, charts, graphs, and special reports and manuals.

Oceanographers may spend some of their time on the water each year gathering data and making observations. Additional oceanographic work is done on dry land by people who only sometimes go to sea. Experiments using models or captive organisms may be conducted in the seaside laboratory.

Oceanographers use equipment designed and manufactured in special shops. This equipment includes devices to measure depths by sound impulses, special thermometers to measure water temperatures, special cameras for underwater photography, and diving gear and machines like the bathyscaphe (a submersible ship for deep-sea exploration). In addition to such commonly used equipment, many new devices have been developed for specific types of underwater work. The oceanographer of the future may be using such tools as a hydraulic miner (a dredge to extract nodules from the ocean floor), an electronic beater (a machine used to drive fish), dye curtains, fish pumps, and instrument buoys. New technologies being developed today include satellite sensors and acoustic current-measuring devices.

The oceanographer is usually part of a highly skilled team, with each member specializing in one of the four main branches of the profession. In actual work, however, there is a tremendous amount of overlap between the four branches. *Biological oceanographers* or *marine biologists* study all aspects of the ocean's plant and animal life. They are interested in how the life develops, interacts, and adapts to its environment. *Physical oceanographers* study such physical aspects of the ocean as temperature and density, waves and currents, and the relationship between the ocean and the atmosphere. *Geological oceanographers* study the topographic features and physical composition of the ocean bottom. Their work greatly contributes to our knowledge and understanding of Earth's history. *Chemical oceanographers* and *marine geochemists* investigate the chemical composition of the water and ocean floor. They may study seawater components, pollutants, and trace chemicals, which are small amounts of dissolved substances that give an area of water a specific quality.

Oceanography jobs can be found all over the United States, and not just where the water meets the shore. Although the majority of jobs are on the Pacific, Atlantic, and Gulf coasts, many other jobs are available to the marine scientist. Universities, colleges, and federal and state agencies are the largest employers of oceanographers.

International organizations, private companies, consulting firms, nonprofit laboratories, and local governments also hire them. Sometimes they are self-employed as consultants with their own businesses.

It is difficult to project what oceanographers of the future may be doing. They may be living and working on the ocean floor. The U.S. Navy Medical Research Laboratory has conducted experiments with people living under 200 feet of water.

REQUIREMENTS

High School

Because a college degree is required for beginning positions in oceanography, you should take four years of college preparatory courses while in high school. Science courses, including geology, biology, and chemistry, and math classes, such as algebra, trigonometry, and statistics, are especially important to take. Because your work will involve a great deal of research and documentation, take English classes to improve your research and communication skills. In addition, take computer science classes because you will be using computers throughout your professional life.

Postsecondary Training

In college, a broad program covering the basic sciences with a major in physics, chemistry, biology, or geology is desirable. In addition, you should include courses in field research or laboratory work in oceanography where available. Graduate work in oceanography is required for most positions in research and teaching. More than 100 institutions offer programs in marine studies, and more than 35 universities have graduate programs leading to a doctoral degree in oceanography.

As a college student preparing for graduate work in oceanography, you should take mathematics through differential and integral calculus and at least one year each of chemistry and physics, biology or geology, and a modern foreign language.

Other Requirements

Personal traits helpful to a career in oceanography are a strong interest in science, particularly the physical and Earth sciences; an interest in situations involving activities of an abstract and creative nature (observing nature, performing experiments, creating objects); an interest in outdoor activities such as hunting, fishing, swimming, boating, or animal care; an interest in scholarly activities (reading, researching, writing); and other interests that cut across the traditional academic boundaries of biology, chemistry, and physics.

You should have above-average aptitudes in verbal, numerical, and spatial abilities. Prospective oceanographers should also be able to discriminate detail among objects in terms of their shape, size, color, or markings.

EXPLORING

Obviously, if you live near coastal regions, you will have an easier time becoming familiar with oceans and ocean life than if you are land-bound. However, some institutions offer work or leisure-time experiences that provide participants with opportunities to explore particular aspects of oceanography. Possible opportunities include work in marine or conservation fisheries or on board seagoing vessels or field experiences in studying rocks, minerals, or aquatic life. If you live or travel near one of the oceanography research centers, such as Woods Hole Oceanographic Institution on Cape Cod, the University of Miami's Institute of Marine Science, or the Scripps Institution of Oceanography in California, you should plan to spend some time learning about their activities and studying their exhibits.

Volunteer work for students is often available with research teams, nonprofit organizations, and public centers such as aquariums. If you do not live near water, try to find summer internships, camps, or programs that involve travel to a coastal area. You can help pave your way into the field by learning all you can about the geology, atmosphere, and plant and animal life of the area where you live, regardless of whether water is present.

EMPLOYERS

Approximately 50 percent of those working in oceanography and marine-related fields work for federal or state governments. Federal employers of oceanographers, ocean engineers, marine technicians, and those interested in marine policy include the Department of Defense, the Environmental Protection Agency, the U.S. Geological Survey, and the National Biological Survey, among others. State governments often employ oceanographers in environmental agencies or state-funded research projects.

Forty percent of oceanographers are employed by colleges or universities, where they teach, conduct research, write, and consult. The remaining 10 percent of oceanographers work for private industries such as oil companies and nonprofit organizations such as environmental societies. An increasing number of oceanographers are being employed each year by industrial firms, particularly those involved in oceanographic instrument and equipment manufacturing, shipbuilding, and chemistry.

STARTING OUT

Most college placement offices are staffed to help you find positions in business and industry after you graduate. Often positions can be found through friends, relatives, or college professors or through the college's placement office by application and interview. College and university assistantships, instructorships, and professorships are usually obtained by recommendation of your major professor or department chairperson. In addition, internships with the government or private industry during college can often lead to permanent employment after graduation. The American Institute of Biological Sciences maintains an employment service and lists both employers and job seekers.

ADVANCEMENT

Starting oceanography positions usually involve working as a laboratory or research assistant, with on-the-job training in applying oceanographic principles to the problems at hand. Some beginning oceanographers with Ph.D.'s may qualify for college teaching or research positions. Experienced personnel, particularly those with advanced graduate work or doctorates, can become supervisors or administrators. Such positions involve considerable responsibility in planning and policy making or policy interpretation. Those who achieve top-level oceanographer positions may plan and supervise research projects involving a number of workers, or they may be in charge of an oceanographic laboratory or aquarium.

EARNINGS

While marine scientists are richly rewarded in nonmaterial ways for their diverse and exciting work with the sea, they almost never become wealthy by American standards. Salaries depend on education, experience, and chosen discipline. Supply and demand issues along with where you work also come into play. Some examples of jobs in the marine sciences that presently pay more than the average include physical oceanography, marine technology and engineering, and computer modeling.

According to a 2000 report by the National Association of Colleges and Employers, students graduating with a bachelor's degree in geology and geological sciences were offered an average starting salary of $35,568. Graduates with a master's degree started at an average of $41,100; with a doctoral degree, $57,500.

According to the *Occupational Outlook Handbook*, in 2000, salaries for geoscientists (which includes geologists, geophysicists, and oceanographers) ranged from less than $33,910 to more than $106,040, with a median of $56,230. The average salary for experienced oceanographers working for the federal government was $71,881.

In addition to their regular salaries, oceanographers may supplement their incomes with fees earned from consulting, lecturing, and publishing their findings. As highly trained scientists, oceanographers usually enjoy good benefits, such as health insurance and retirement plans offered by their employers.

WORK ENVIRONMENT

Oceanographers in shore stations, laboratories, and research centers work five-day, 40-hour weeks. Occasionally, they serve a longer shift, particularly when a research experiment demands around-the-clock surveillance. Such assignments may also involve unusual working hours, depending on the nature of the research or the purpose of the trip. Trips at sea mean time away from home for periods extending from a few days to several months. Sea expeditions may be physically demanding and present an entirely different way of life: living on board a ship. Weather conditions may impose some hazards during these assignments. Choosing to engage in underwater research may mean a more adventuresome and hazardous way of life than in other occupations. It is wise to discover early whether or not life at sea appeals to you so that you may pursue appropriate jobs within the oceanography field.

Many jobs in oceanography, however, exist in laboratories, offices, and aquariums, with little time spent underwater or at sea. Many oceanographers are needed to analyze samples brought to land from sea; to plan, develop, and organize seafaring trips from land; and to teach. Oceanographers who work in colleges or universities get the added benefit of the academic calendar, which provides time off for travel or research.

OUTLOOK

The U.S. Department of Labor expects employment for oceanographers to grow about as fast as the average through 2010. Although the field of marine science is growing, researchers specializing in the popular field of biological oceanography, or marine biology, will face competition for available positions and research funding over the next few years. However, funding for graduate students and professional positions is expected to increase during the coming decade in the areas of global climate change, environmental research and management, fisheries science, and marine biomedical and pharmaceutical research programs. Although job availability is difficult to predict for several years out, anyone doing good, strong academic work with a well-known professor in the field has good chances for employment.

In the late 1990s, the largest demand in oceanography and marine-related fields was for physical and chemical oceanographers and ocean engineers, according to the Oceanography Society. Demand and supply, however, are difficult to predict and can change according to the world market situation; for example, the state of the offshore oil market can affect demand for geological and geophysical oceanographers.

The march of technology will continue to create and expand job opportunities for those interested in the marine sciences. As ways of collecting and analyzing data become more advanced, many more research positions are opening up for microbiologists, geneticists, and biochemists, fields that were limited by the capabilities of past technology but are now rapidly expanding. All these fields can have ties to the marine biological sciences. In general, oceanographers who also have training in other sciences or in engineering will probably have better opportunities for employment than those with training limited to oceanography.

The Oceanography Society says the growing interest in understanding and protecting the environment will also create new jobs. Careers related to fisheries resources, including basic research in biology and chemistry, as well as mariculture and sea ranching, will also increase. Because the oceans hold vast resources of commercially valuable minerals, employment opportunities will come from pharmaceutical and biotechnology companies and others interested in mining these substances for potential "miracle drugs" and other commercial uses. Continued deep-sea exploration made possible by underwater robotics and autonomous seacraft may also create more market opportunities for underwater research, with perhaps more international than U.S.-based employment potential.

FOR MORE INFORMATION

For education and career information, contact the following organizations:

Acoustical Society of America
2 Huntington Quadrangle, Suite 1NO1
Melville, NY 11747-4502
Tel: 516-576-2360
Email: asa@aip.org
http://asa.aip.org

American Geophysical Union
2000 Florida Avenue, NW
Washington, DC 20009-1277
Tel: 800-966-2481
Email: service@agu.org
http://www.agu.org

The education and outreach section of the AIBS website has information on a number of careers in biology.

American Institute of Biological Sciences (AIBS)
1444 Eye Street, NW, Suite 200
Washington, DC 20005
Tel: 202-628-1500
Email: admin@aibs.org
http://www.aibs.org

Visit the ASLO's website for information on careers and education. For information on membership and publications, contact

American Society of Limnology and Oceanography (ASLO)
5400 Bosque Boulevard, Suite 680
Waco, TX 76710-4446
Tel: 800-929-2756
Email: business@aslo.org
http://www.aslo.org

For information about ocean careers and education, contact

Department of Oceanography
Texas A&M University

3146 TAMU
College Station, TX 77843-3146
Tel: 979-845-7211
http://www-ocean.tamu.edu

Visit the MTS website for scholarship information and to order the booklet Education and Training Programs in Oceanography and Related Fields.
Marine Technology Society (MTS)
5565 Sterrett Place, Suite 108
Columbia, MD 21044
Tel: 410-884-5330
http://www.mtsociety.org

Contact this society for ocean news and information on membership.
Oceanography Society
PO Box 1931
Rockville, MD 20849-1931
Tel: 301-251-7708
Email: info@tos.org
http://www.tos.org

For information on undergraduate and graduate programs available at Scripps Institution of Oceanography, contact
Scripps Institution of Oceanography
University of California, San Diego
9500 Gilman Drive
La Jolla, CA 92093
Tel: 858-534-3624
http://www-sio.ucsd.edu

The Scripps Institution of Oceanography Library provides numerous links to career information at this website.
Careers in Oceanography, Marine Science, and Marine Biology
http://scilib.ucsd.edu/sio/guide/career.html

INTERVIEW

Mary Batteen is the chairperson of the oceanography department at the Naval Postgraduate School (NPS) in Monterey, California, a professor in the department, and a working oceanographer. She spoke with the editors of Careers in Focus: Environment *about her job and the field of oceanography in general.*

Q. Please describe the primary and secondary responsibilities of your job, as well as your major research interests.

A. Besides running the oceanography department, which has around 40 tenure-track and research professors/faculty, around 25 technical staff, and four office staff, I teach graduate-level oceanography courses, advise graduate students on their M.S./Ph.D. theses/dissertations, and carry out research studies.

My major research interest is understanding the coastal circulation off west coasts like California, Portugal, Morocco, Chile, and Western Australia. Typical research questions I pursue are: Why, at the same latitude, is the water warm off Western Australia and cool off the other west coasts? Why do some coastal currents flow opposite to the prevailing winds? What roles do wind forcing, capes (bays), and bottom topography play in causing eddies to develop off west coasts? To address these questions, I use a combination of numerical models and available ocean observations.

Q. What is a typical work day like for you? Do your responsibilities and/or interactions vary greatly?

A. As you can see from my typical work schedule below, my responsibilities and interactions vary greatly. As the chairperson, I interact regularly with a variety of people: my office staff, faculty, technical staff (usually oceanographers with M.S. degrees), other chairs, the dean, the provost, and many students. I am responsible for making sure that the oceanography department runs smoothly. As a faculty member, I regularly interact with students when I teach, advise theses, or carry out joint research with them.

Typical work day:

8:00 A.M. Check email and my inbox and answer the most pressing ones right away. Set up work schedule with the office staff.

8:30 A.M. Prepare lecture for class. A typical lecture might be: Why is the ocean salty?

9:30 A.M. Teach my class. Give out study guide questions to elicit students questions while I am lecturing. Engage students in discussion of possible answers to the questions while lecturing.

10:30 A.M. Read and comment on proposals written by faculty to be sent to National Science Foundation.

11:00 A.M. Have a meeting with a thesis student. Discuss which figures he/she has worked on that best illustrate the scientific points they are trying to make.

12:00 P.M. Lunchtime! Go for a walk at the beach or around the NPS lake.

1:00 P.M. Work on a research paper for publication in a refereed oceanography journal.

2:00 P.M. Check current research results, which may include output from a numerical model on the ocean circulation in the Gulf of Cadiz.

3:00 P.M. Have a faculty meeting and discuss upcoming teaching schedules and oceanography cruises.

4:00 P.M. Attend an oceanography seminar and learn about the latest research on marine geodesy, whale tracking, etc.

Q. What is your work environment like? Does your job involve travel?

A. Although I have my own office, I constantly interact with all types of people either directly, through email, or on the phone. I use my PC and laptop much of the day and compose answers to requests that range from finding people to go out on cruises to getting information on some oceanography topic.

My job has always involved much travel. Even as a graduate student, I went on oceanography cruises off Peru for 45 days at a time. Nowadays I travel frequently to the East Coast (particularly to Washington, D.C.) to see our funding agents, our sponsors, and to speak about oceanography at educational institutions such as MIT and the Naval Academy. I also attend and give presentations at several national oceanography meetings each year in places such as Los Angeles, Portland (Oregon), and Honolulu.

Q. What are the expectations people typically have as they enter the field of oceanography? Would you say the realities are much different?

A. Most oceanographers, particularly biological ones, are quite surprised to learn that greater computer and math skills can enhance their job opportunities. Initially most people expect that their jobs will involve much diving and/or going on scientific cruises. Since much of oceanography data is now collected remotely, say by drifters, and the information is automatically sent to satellites, there is a need for oceanographers who can analyze the oceanographic data and use models of the ocean to try to predict the ocean circulation.

Q. What course of study did you pursue during and after college? Did it prepare you for your career?

A. Although I became interested in oceanography when I was a teenager, I found out that oceanography was primarily a graduate field. As a result, I studied a broad range of science and math in college, which prepared me to get into graduate school. I then depended on my graduate student work experiences to help me to decide what aspect of oceanography I wanted to focus on. After extensive cruises to Peru doing fieldwork and getting a bit seasick, I decided that running numerical models of the ocean circulation was preferable for me. I made this the topic of my Ph.D. dissertation and have been working in this area ever since.

Q. Did you complete any internships or special training for this career?

A. Yes. I was a graduate teaching assistant while pursuing my M.S. degree in oceanography. Besides learning to teach, I learned on-the-job skills while out on oceanography cruises. While pursuing my Ph.D. I was a graduate research assistant. I learned many computer skills while analyzing oceanographic data and running numerical models. After receiving my Ph.D. I received a National Research Associateship (NRC) from the National Academy of Sciences, which allowed me to come to NPS to begin focusing on west coast oceanography.

Q. What other types of positions have you held?

A. At NPS I have held the following faculty positions: adjunct professor, assistant professor, and associate professor. Prior to being the chairperson, I was the associate chair for academic affairs and the academic associate for the following curricula/programs: basic oceanography, operational oceanography, and meteorology and oceanography.

Q. What is the current outlook for growth and advancement in your field?

A. For technical support in oceanography, the current outlook today is very bright. For example, students coming from programs such as MATE (Marine Advanced Technology Education), an NSF-sponsored program, are exposed to a fine combination of courses and on-the-job training. The future also looks promising for oceanographers with good computer skills who have an M.S. or Ph.D. and who are interested in working in federal labs, such as the Fleet Numerical Meteorology and Oceanography Center in Monterey, California. Although academic careers are presently a bit hard to find in all scientific fields due to a shortage of math and science majors, hopefully this will change as the importance of the ocean is being brought to the public's attention around the world. Many universities are beginning to offer undergraduate degrees in oceanography and other environmental sciences, which should lead to future academic careers in oceanography.

Q. What would you say are the most important skills and personal qualities for someone in your career?

A. An important attribute is to always be willing to learn and to stay current in oceanography developments. Another important skill for an instructor is to teach as you yourself would like to be taught. This keeps you from being a stuffy teacher who only lectures. Students should feel free to ask questions, to interact with the instructor, and to get excited about the material being presented.

As an oceanographer I try to think of the next research question I would like to answer and then work on addressing this question. I make sure I regularly attend conferences/workshops and give presentations so that I can stay current in the field. A career in oceanography is one that allows you to explore many unanswered questions in a relatively young field. Getting paid for work that you can't help but enjoy is great, whether you are out at sea or are an armchair oceanographer.

Q. What advice would you give to someone who is interested in pursuing a career in oceanography?

A. While still in school, find out what aspect of oceanography you are most interested in and get a broad technical background in engineering, science, math, computer science, and technical writing. Go to a library at a university that has published job announcements available and regularly find out what additional skills (such as MATLAB and C++ programming) are being asked for in oceanography jobs, then try to obtain these additional skills while in college. If you get into graduate school, try to also obtain some graduate support and regularly attend national oceanography meetings such as Ocean Sciences to see what is going on in the field.

Lastly, continue to think of oceanography as a wonderful and thrilling field. Whatever job you obtain in oceanography, you will find yourself surrounded by others who truly enjoy their jobs, particularly since so much is being discovered every day in this blossoming field.

Park Rangers

OVERVIEW

Park rangers enforce laws and regulations in national, state, and county parks. They help care for and maintain parks as well as inform, guide, and ensure the safety of park visitors.

HISTORY

The National Park System in the United States was begun by Congress in 1872 with the creation of Yellowstone National Park. The National Park Service (NPS), a bureau of the U.S. Department of the Interior, was created in 1916 to preserve, protect, and manage the national, cultural, historical, and recreational areas of the National Park System. At that time, the park system contained less than 1 million acres. Today, the country's national parks cover more than 80.7 million acres of mountains, plains, deserts, swamps, historic sites, lakeshores, forests, rivers, battlefields, memorials, archaeological properties, and recreation areas.

All NPS areas are given one of the following designations: National Park, National Historical Park, National Battlefield, National Battlefield Park, National Battlefield Site, National Military Site, National Memorial, National Historic Site, National Monument, National Preserve, National Seashore, National Parkway, National Lakeshore, National Reserve, National River, National Wild and Scenic River, National Recreation Area, or just Park. (The White House in Washington, D.C., for example, which is administered by the NPS, is officially a Park.)

To protect the fragile, irreplaceable resources located in these areas, and to protect the millions of visitors who climb, ski, hike, boat, fish, and otherwise explore them, the National Park Service employs park rangers. State and county parks employ rangers to perform similar tasks.

THE JOB

Park rangers have a wide variety of duties that range from conservation efforts to bookkeeping. Their first responsibility, however, is safety. Rangers who work in parks with treacherous terrain, dangerous wildlife, or severe weather must make sure hikers, campers, and backpackers follow outdoor safety codes. They often require visitors to register at park offices so that rangers will know when someone does not return from a hike or climb and may be hurt. Rangers often participate in search-and-rescue missions for visitors who are lost or injured in parks. In mountainous or forested regions, they may use helicopters or horses for searches.

Rangers also protect parks from inappropriate use and other threats from humans. They register vehicles and collect parking and registration fees, which are used to help maintain roads and facilities. They enforce the laws, regulations, and policies of the parks, patrolling to prevent vandalism, theft, and harm to wildlife. Rangers may arrest and evict people who violate these laws. Some of their efforts to conserve and protect park resources include keeping jeeps and other motorized vehicles off sand dunes and other fragile lands. They make sure visitors do not litter, pollute water, chop down trees for firewood, or start unsafe campfires that could lead to catastrophic forest fires. When forest fires do start, rangers often help with the dangerous, arduous task of putting them out.

Park rangers carry out various tasks associated with the management of the natural resources within our National Park System. An important aspect of this responsibility is the care and management of both native and exotic animal species found within the boundaries of the parks. Duties may include conducting basic research, as well as disseminating information about the reintroduction of native animal populations and the protection of the natural habitat that supports the animals.

Rangers also help with conservation, research, and ecology efforts that are not connected to visitors' use of the park. They may study wildlife behavior patterns, for example, by tagging and following certain animals. In this way, they can chart the animals' migration patterns, assess the animals' impact on the park's ecosystem, and determine whether the park should take measures to control or encourage certain wildlife populations.

Some rangers study plant life and may work with conservationists to reintroduce native or endangered species. They measure the qual-

A park ranger in Monterey Bay, California, teaches students about tide pools. *(Corbis)*

ity of water and air in the park to monitor and mitigate the effects of pollution and other threats from sources outside park boundaries.

In addition, park rangers help visitors enjoy and experience parks. In historical and other cultural parks, such as the Alamo in San Antonio, Independence Hall in Philadelphia, and the Lincoln Home in Springfield, Illinois, rangers give lectures and provide guided tours explaining the history and significance of the site. In natural parks, they may lecture on conservation topics, provide information about plants and animals in the park, and take visitors on interpretive walks, pointing out the area's flora, fauna, and geological character-istics. At a Civil War battlefield park, such as Gettysburg National Military Park in Pennsylvania or Vicksburg National Military Park in Mississippi, they explain to visitors what happened at that site dur-ing the Civil War and its implications for our country.

Park rangers are also indispensable to the management and admin-istration of parks. They issue permits to visitors and vehicles and help plan the recreational activities in parks. They help in the planning and managing of park budgets. They keep records and compile statistics concerning weather conditions, resource conservation activities, and the number of park visitors.

Many rangers supervise other workers in the parks who build and maintain park facilities, work part time or seasonally, or operate concession facilities. Rangers often have their own park maintenance responsibilities, such as trail building, landscaping, and caring for visitor centers.

In some parks, rangers are specialists in certain areas of park protection, safety, or management. For example, in areas with heavy snowfalls and a high incidence of avalanches, experts in avalanche control and snow safety are designated *snow rangers*. They monitor snow conditions and patrol park areas to make sure visitors are not lost in snowslides.

REQUIREMENTS

High School

To prepare for the necessary college course load, you should take courses in Earth science, biology, mathematics, English, and speech. Any classes or activities that deal with plant and animal life, the weather, geography, and interacting with others will be helpful.

Postsecondary Training

Employment as a federal or state park ranger requires either a college degree or a specific amount of education and experience. Approximately 200 colleges and universities offer bachelor's degree programs in park management and park recreation. To meet employment requirements, students in other relevant college programs must accumulate at least 24 semester hours of academic credit in park recreation and management, history, behavioral sciences, forestry, botany, geology, or other applicable subject areas.

Without a degree, you will need three years of experience in parks or conservation and you must show an understanding of what is required in park work. In addition, you must demonstrate good communications skills. A combination of education and experience can also fulfill job requirements, with one academic year of study equaling nine months of experience. Also, the orientation and training a ranger receives on the job may be supplemented with formal training courses.

To succeed as a ranger, you will need skills in protecting forests, parks, and wildlife and in interpreting natural or historical resources. Law enforcement and management skills are also important. If you wish to move into management positions, you may need a graduate degree. Approximately 50 universities offer master's degrees in park recreation and management and 16 have doctoral programs.

Other Requirements

In order to be a good park ranger, you should believe in the importance of the country's park resources and the mission of the park system. If you enjoy working outdoors, independently and with others, you may enjoy park ranger work. Rangers need self-confidence, patience, and the ability to stay levelheaded during emergencies. To participate in rescues, you need courage, physical stamina, and endurance, and to deal with visitors you must have tact, sincerity, a personable nature, and a sense of humor. A sense of camaraderie among fellow rangers also can add to the enjoyment of being a park ranger.

EXPLORING

If you are interested in exploring park ranger work, you may wish to apply for part-time or seasonal work in national, state, or county parks. Such workers usually perform maintenance and other unskilled tasks, but they have opportunities to observe park rangers and talk with them about their work. You might also choose to work as a volunteer. Many park research activities, study projects, and rehabilitation efforts are conducted by volunteer groups affiliated with universities or conservation organizations, and these activities can provide insight into the work done by park rangers.

EMPLOYERS

Park rangers in the National Park Service are employed by the U.S. Department of the Interior. Other rangers may be employed by other federal agencies or by state and county agencies in charge of their respective parks.

STARTING OUT

Many workers enter national park ranger jobs after working part time or seasonally at different parks. These workers often work at information desks or in fire control or law enforcement positions. Some help maintain trails, collect trash, or perform forestry activities. If you are interested in applying for a park ranger job with the federal government, contact your local Federal Job Information Center or the Federal Office of Personnel Management in Washington, D.C., for application information. To find jobs in state parks, you should write to the appropriate state departments for information.

ADVANCEMENT

Nearly all rangers start in entry-level positions, which means that nearly all higher level openings are filled by the promotion of current workers. Entry-level rangers may move into positions as district ranger or park manager, or they may become specialists in resource management or park planning. Rangers who show management skills and become park managers may move into administrative positions in the district, regional, or national headquarters.

The orientation and training a ranger receives on the job may be supplemented with formal training courses. Training for job skills unique to the National Park Service is available at the Horace M. Albright Training Center at Grand Canyon National Park in Arizona and the Stephen T. Mather Training Center at Harpers Ferry, West Virginia. In addition, training is available at the Federal Law Enforcement Training Center in Brunswick, Georgia.

EARNINGS

Rangers in the National Park Service are usually hired at the GS-5 grade level, with a base salary of $23,442 in 2003. More experienced or educated rangers may enter the Park Service at the GS-9 level, which pays $35,519 to start. The average ranger is generally at about the second step of the GS-7 level, which translated to a salary of $30,005 in 2003. The most experienced rangers can earn $35,813, the highest salary step in the G-7 level.

To move beyond this level, most rangers must become supervisors, subdistrict rangers, district rangers, or division chiefs. At these higher levels, people can earn over $80,000 per year. These positions are difficult to obtain, however, because the turnover rate for positions above the GS-7 level is exceptionally low. The government may provide housing to rangers who work in remote areas.

Rangers in state parks work for the state government. They receive comparable salaries and benefits, including paid vacations, sick leave, paid holidays, health and life insurance, and pension plans.

WORK ENVIRONMENT

Rangers work in parks all over the country, from the Okefenokee Swamp in Florida to the Rocky Mountains of Colorado. They work in the mountains and forests of Hawaii, Alaska, and California and in urban and suburban parks throughout the United States.

National park rangers are hired to work 40 hours per week, but their actual working hours can be long and irregular, with a great deal of overtime. They may receive extra pay or time off for working overtime. Some rangers are on call 24 hours a day for emergencies. During the peak tourist seasons, rangers work longer hours. Although many rangers work in offices, many also work outside in all kinds of climates and weather, and most work in a combination of the two settings. Workers may be called upon to risk their own health to rescue injured visitors in cold, snow, rain, and darkness. Rangers in Alaska must adapt to long daylight hours in the summer and short daylight hours in the winter. Working outdoors in beautiful surroundings, however, can be wonderfully stimulating and rewarding for the right kind of worker.

OUTLOOK

Park ranger jobs are scarce and competition for them is fierce. The National Park Service has reported that the ratio of applicants to available positions is sometimes as high as one hundred to one. As a result, applicants should attain the greatest number and widest variety of applicable skills possible. They may wish to study subjects they can use in other fields: forestry, land management, conservation, wildlife management, history, and natural sciences, for example.

The scarcity of openings is expected to continue indefinitely. Job seekers, therefore, may wish to apply for outdoor work with agencies other than the National Park Service, including other federal land and resource management agencies and similar state and local agencies. Such agencies usually have more openings.

FOR MORE INFORMATION

For information on federal employment, contact
Federal Job Information Center
Office of Personnel Management
1900 E Street, NW, Room 1416
Washington, DC 20415
Email: usajobshelp@opm.gov
http://www.usajobs.opm.gov

For general career information, contact the following organizations:
National Association of State Park Directors
9894 East Holden Place
Tucson, AZ 85748
Tel: 520-298-4924
Email: naspdglen@cox.net
http://www.naspd.org

National Parks Conservation Association
1300 19th Street, NW, Suite 300
Washington, DC 20036

Email: npca@npca.org
http://www.npca.org

National Recreation and Park Association
22377 Belmont Ridge Road
Ashburn, VA 20148-4501
Tel: 703-858-0784
Email: info@nrpa.org
http://www.nrpa.org

Student Conservation Association
689 River Road
PO Box 550
Charlestown, NH 03603-0550
Tel: 603-543-1700
http://www.thesca.org

For information about careers, job openings, and national parks, contact
National Park Service
1849 C Street, NW
Washington, DC 20240
Tel: 202-208-6843
http://www.nps.gov

Range Managers

OVERVIEW

Range managers work to maintain and improve grazing lands on public and private property. They research, develop, and carry out methods to improve and increase the production of forage plants, livestock, and wildlife without damaging the environment; develop and carry out plans for water facilities, erosion control, and soil treatments; restore rangelands that have been damaged by fire, pests, and undesirable plants; and manage the upkeep of range improvements, such as fences, corrals, and reservoirs.

HISTORY

Early in the history of the world, primitive peoples grazed their livestock wherever forage was plentiful. As the supply of grass and shrubs became depleted, they simply moved on, leaving the stripped land to suffer the effects of soil erosion. When civilization grew and the nomadic tribes began to establish settlements, people began to recognize the need for conservation and developed simple methods of land terracing, irrigation, and the rotation of grazing lands.

Much the same thing happened in the United States. The rapid expansion across the continent in the 19th century was accompanied by the destruction of plant and animal life and the abuse of the soil. Because the country's natural resources appeared inexhaustible, the cries of alarm that came from a few concerned conservationists went unheeded. It was not until after 1890 that conservation became a national policy. Today several state and federal agencies are actively involved in protecting the nation's soil, water, forests, and wildlife.

QUICK FACTS

School Subjects
Biology
Earth science

Personal Skills
Leadership/management
Technical/scientific

Work Environment
Indoors and outdoors
Primarily multiple locations

Minimum Education Level
Bachelor's degree

Salary Range
$23,776 to $50,715 to $61,451+

Certification or Licensing
Voluntary

Outlook
Little change or more slowly than the average

DOT
040

GOE
02.02.02

NOC
2223

O*NET-SOC
19-1031.02

Rangelands cover more than a billion acres of the United States, mostly in the western states and Alaska. Many natural resources are found there: grass and shrubs for animal grazing, wildlife habitats, water from vast watersheds, recreation facilities, and valuable mineral and energy resources. In addition, rangelands are used by scientists who conduct studies of the environment.

THE JOB

Range managers are sometimes known as *range scientists, range ecologists*, or *range conservationists*. Their goal is to maximize range resources without damaging the environment. They accomplish this in a number of ways.

To help ranchers attain optimum livestock production, range managers study the rangelands to determine the number and kind of livestock that can be most profitably grazed, the grazing system to use, and the best seasons for grazing. The system they recommend must be designed to conserve the soil and vegetation for other uses, such as wildlife habitats, outdoor recreation, and timber.

Grazing lands must continually be restored and improved. Range managers study plants to determine which varieties are best suited to a particular range and to develop improved methods for reseeding. They devise biological, chemical, or mechanical ways of controlling undesirable and poisonous plants, and they design methods of protecting the range from grazing damage.

Range managers also develop and help carry out plans for water facilities, structures for erosion control, and soil treatments. They are responsible for the construction and maintenance of such improvements as fencing, corrals, and reservoirs for stock watering.

Although a great deal of range managers' time is spent outdoors, they also spend some time in offices, consulting with other conservation specialists, preparing written reports, and doing administrative work.

Rangelands have more than one use, so range managers often work in such closely related fields as wildlife and watershed management, forest management, and recreation. *Soil conservationists* and *naturalists* are concerned with maintaining ecological balance both on the range and in the forest preserves.

REQUIREMENTS
High School
If you are interested in pursuing a career in range management, you should begin planning your education early. Since you will need a col-

lege degree for this work, take college preparatory classes in high school. Your class schedule should include the sciences, such as Earth science, biology, and chemistry. Take mathematics and economics classes. Any courses that teach you to work with a computer will also be beneficial. You will frequently use this tool in your career to keep records, file reports, and do planning. English courses will also help you develop your research, writing, and reading skills. You will need all of these skills in college and beyond.

Postsecondary Training

The minimum educational requirement for range managers is usually a bachelor's degree in range management or range science. To be hired by the federal government, you will need at least 42 credit hours in plant, animal, or soil sciences and natural resources management courses, including at least 18 hours in range management. If you would like a teaching or research position, you will need a graduate degree in range management. Advanced degrees may also prove helpful for advancement in other jobs.

To receive a bachelor's degree in range management, students must have acquired a basic knowledge of biology, chemistry, physics, mathematics, and communication skills. Specialized courses in range management combine plant, animal, and soil sciences with the principles of ecology and resource management. Students are also encouraged to take electives, such as economics, forestry, hydrology, agronomy, wildlife, and computer science.

While a number of schools offer some courses related to range management, only about 35 colleges and universities have degree programs in range management or range science or in a discipline with a range management or range science option.

Certification or Licensing

The Society for Range Management offers certification as a Certified Range Management Consultant (CRMC) or a Certified Professional in Rangeland Management (CPRM). These are voluntary certifications but demonstrate a professional's commitment to the field and the high quality of his or her work. Requirements include having a bachelor's degree and at least five years of experience in the field as well as passing a written exam.

Other Requirements

Along with their technical skills, range managers must be able to speak and write effectively and to work well with others. Range managers need to be self-motivated and flexible. They are generally persons who do not want the restrictions of an office setting and a rigid schedule. They should have a love for the outdoors as well as good health and physical stamina for the strenuous activity that this occupation requires.

EXPLORING

As a high school student, you can test your appetite for outdoor work by applying for summer jobs on ranches or farms. Other ways of exploring this occupation include a field trip to a ranch or interviews with or lectures by range managers, ranchers, or conservationists. Any volunteer work with conservation organizations—large or small—will give you an idea of what range managers do and will help you when you apply to colleges and for employment.

As a college student, you can get more direct experience by applying for summer jobs in range management with such federal agencies as the Forest Service, the Natural Resource Conservation Service (NRCS), and the Bureau of Land Management (BLM). This experience may better qualify you for jobs when you graduate.

EMPLOYERS

The majority of range managers are employed by the federal government in the BLM or the NRCS. State governments employ range managers in game and fish departments, state land agencies, and extension services.

In private industry, the number of range managers is increasing. They work for coal and oil companies to help reclaim mined areas, for banks and real estate firms to help increase the revenue from landholdings, and for private consulting firms and large ranches. Some range managers with advanced degrees teach and do research at colleges and universities. Others work overseas with U.S. and U.N. agencies and with foreign governments.

STARTING OUT

The usual way to enter this occupation is to apply directly to the appropriate government agencies. People interested in working for the federal government may contact the Department of Agriculture's Forest Service or the NRCS, or the Department of the Interior's Bureau of Indian Affairs or the BLM. Others may apply to local state employment offices for jobs in state land agencies, game and fish departments, or agricultural extension services. Your college placement office should have listings of available jobs.

ADVANCEMENT

Range managers may advance to administrative positions in which they plan and supervise the work of others and write reports. Others may go into teaching or research. An advanced degree is often necessary for the higher level jobs in this field. Another way for range managers to advance is to enter business for themselves as *range management consultants* or *ranchers*.

EARNINGS

According to the U.S. Department of Labor, in 2001, most bachelor's degree graduates entering federal government jobs as foresters, range managers, or soil conservationists started at $23,776 or $30,035, depending on academic achievement. Those with a master's degree could start at $30,035 or $42,783, and those with doctorates could start at $52,162 or, in research positions, at $61,451. The average federal salary for rangeland managers was $50,715 in 2001.

State governments and private companies pay their range managers salaries that are about the same as those paid by the federal government. Range managers are also eligible for paid vacations and sick days, health and life insurance, and other benefits.

WORK ENVIRONMENT

Range managers, particularly those just beginning their careers, spend a great deal of time on the range. That means they must work outdoors in all kinds of weather. They usually travel by car or small plane, but in rough country they use four-wheel-drive vehicles or get around on horseback or on foot. When riding the range, managers may spend a considerable amount of time away from home, and the work is often quite strenuous.

As range managers advance to administrative jobs, they spend more time working in offices, writing reports, and planning and supervising the work of others. Range managers may work alone or under direct supervision; often they work as part of a team. In any case, they must deal constantly with people—not only their superiors and co-workers but with the general public, ranchers, government officials, and other conservation specialists.

OUTLOOK

This is a small occupation, and most of the openings will arise when older, experienced range managers retire or leave the occupation. The

U.S. Department of Labor predicts that job growth will be slower than the average through 2010 for conservation scientists and foresters, a category that includes range managers. The need for range managers should be stimulated by a growing demand for wildlife habitats, recreation, and water as well as by an increasing concern for the environment. A greater number of large ranches will employ range managers to improve range management practices and increase output and profitability. Range specialists will also be employed in larger numbers by private industry to reclaim lands damaged by oil and coal exploration. A small number of new jobs will result from the need for range and soil conservationists to provide technical assistance to owners of grazing land through the NRCS.

An additional demand for range managers could be created by the conversion of rangelands to other purposes, such as wildlife habitats and recreation. Federal employment for these activities, however, depends on the passage of legislation concerning the management of range resources, an area that is always controversial. Smaller budgets may also limit employment growth in this area.

FOR MORE INFORMATION

Career and education information may be obtained from
National Recreation and Park Association
22377 Belmont Ridge Road
Ashburn, VA 20148
Tel: 703-858-0784
Email: info@nrpa.org
http://www.nrpa.org

This organization has career, education, scholarship, and certification information. Student membership is also available through its International Student Conclave.
Society for Range Management
445 Union Boulevard, Suite 230
Lakewood, CO 80228
Tel: 303-986-3309
http://www.rangelands.org

For information about career opportunities in the federal government, contact
U.S. Department of Agriculture
Natural Resources Conservation Service
PO Box 2890

Washington, DC 20013
http://www.nrcs.usda.gov

U.S. Department of Agriculture
U.S. Forest Service
PO Box 96090
Washington, D.C. 20090-6090
http://www.fs.fed.us

U.S. Department of the Interior
Bureau of Indian Affairs
1849 C Street, NW
Washington, DC 20240
Tel: 202-208-3100
http://www.doi.gov

U.S. Department of the Interior
Bureau of Land Management
1849 C Street, NW, Room 406-LS
Washington, DC 20240
Tel: 202-452-5125
http://www.blm.gov

U.S. Department of the Interior
National Park Service
1849 C Street, NW
Washington, DC 20240
Tel: 202-208-5391
http://www.nps.gov

Recycling Coordinators

OVERVIEW

Recycling coordinators manage recycling programs for city, county, or state governments or large organizations, such as colleges or military bases. They work with waste haulers and material recovery facilities, to arrange for collecting, sorting, and processing recyclables such as aluminum, glass, and paper, from households and businesses. Recycling coordinators are often responsible for educating the public about the value of recycling as well as instructing residents on how to properly separate recyclables in their homes. Recycling coordinators keep records of recycling rates in their municipality and help set goals for diversion of recyclables from the waste stream.

HISTORY

Recycling coordinators have a brief history in the job as it is known today. Only in the 1980s and early 1990s did many states begin setting recycling goals, creating the need for recycling coordinators at the local level. Prior to that time, private citizen groups or industry led most recycling efforts, so there was little need for municipal recycling coordinators. While much of today's recycling is driven by a desire to improve the environment, earlier recycling was often driven by economic forces. During the Great Depression, individual citizens or groups, such as the Boy Scouts, held newspaper drives and turned the newspaper over to a recycler. The recycler paid a minimal amount for the collection of the newspapers and then generally sold the newspaper to industry, which recycled or otherwise reused the newspaper. During World War II, shortages in raw materials to support the war prompted citizens to hold drives for aluminum, rubber, paper, and scrap metal; this time the spirit of recycling was patriotic as well as economic.

Other than times of shortage, governments had little concern for how people disposed of waste, simply because there was relatively little waste. Municipalities had been dumping, burning, burying, or otherwise disposing of residents' waste for years with little consequence. In 1898, New York City opened the first garbage-sorting plant in the United States, recycling some of the trash. The first aluminum recycling plants were built in the early 1900s in Chicago and Cleveland. By the 1920s, about 70 percent of U.S. cities had limited recycling programs, according to the League of Women Voters.

Can buybacks began in the 1950s; newspaper was first recycled in 1961 by a mill in New Jersey. By 1960, the United States recycled about 7 percent of its municipal waste. In the mid-1960s, the federal government began to take greater interest in municipal waste-handling methods. Part of the Solid Waste Disposal Act of 1965 granted money for states to develop waste-handling programs. The Resource Conservation and Recovery Act of 1970 and 1976 amendments defined types of municipal solid waste (MSW) and spelled out minimum standards for waste handling.

State and federal governments, such as branches of the Environmental Protection Agency, were the earliest to hire people who specialized in recycling. These recycling experts usually acted in an advisory capacity to local governments that were trying to develop their own programs.

In the 1990s, more states began to set recycling goals, driving the increase in need for recycling coordinators. By 1998, all but six states had set formal recycling goals. These goals are generally stated in terms of the percentage of waste to be diverted from ending up in a landfill. Most states set goals between 20 and 50 percent. To encourage counties to make the effort at a local level, many state governments offered grants to counties to fund new recycling programs, and many counties found they needed a full-time person to coordinate the new effort. Initially, only the most populous counties qualified for the grants to afford a recycling program because they could divert the highest volume from landfills.

THE JOB

As recycling becomes more widespread, fewer recycling coordinators are faced with the task of organizing a municipal program from scratch. Instead, recycling coordinators work to improve current recycling rates in several ways. While recycling coordinators spend some time on administrative tasks, such as meeting with waste haulers and government officials and writing reports, they often need a considerable amount of time for public-education efforts. One recycling coordinator in North Dakota notes that only a small portion of the average recycling coordinator's job is spent sitting behind a desk.

Educating the public on proper separation of recyclables as well as explaining the need for recycling are a large part of a recycling coordinator's job. Good oral communication skills are essential for a recycling coordinator to succeed in this role. Getting people who haven't recycled before to start doing so can take some convincing. Recycling coordinators spread their message by speaking to community groups, businesses, and schools. They use persuasive speaking skills to urge people to do the extra work peeling labels from and washing bottles and jars instead of just throwing them out, and separating newspapers, magazines, cardboard, and other types of paper. Even as recycling increases in this country, many people are accustomed to disposing of trash as quickly as possible without giving it a second thought. It is the task of a recycling coordinator to get people to change such habits, and how well a recycling coordinator is able to do this can make the difference in the success of the entire program.

In some communities, recycling coordinators have economics on their side when it comes to getting people to change their habits. In so-called pay-as-you-throw programs, residents pay for garbage disposal based on how much waste their household produces. So recycling, although it may mean extra work, makes sense because it saves the homeowner money. For example, residents may be charged extra for any waste they set out at the curb beyond one garbage can per week. In communities with these programs, recycling rates tend to be higher, and recycling coordinators have an easier task of convincing people to recycle. Another part of a recycling coordinator's role as educator is answering questions about how recyclables are to be separated. Especially with new programs, residents often have questions about separating recyclables, such as what type of paper can be set out with newspaper, whether labels should be peeled from jars, and even keeping track of which week of the month or day of the week they should set their recyclables out with the trash. Fielding these types of calls always demands some portion of a recycling coordinator's time.

Most recycling coordinators spend a minimal amount of time on record keeping, perhaps 5 percent, one coordinator estimates. The coordinator is responsible for making monthly, or sometimes quarterly, reports to state and federal government agencies. Recycling coordinators also fill out grant applications for state and federal funding to improve their programs.

Some recycling coordinators work on military bases or college campuses. The goal of a recycling coordinator who works in one of these settings is the same as a municipal recycling coordinator—getting people to recycle; how they go about it may differ. The recycling coordinator on a college campus, for example, has a new set of residents every year to educate about the college's recycling program.

Recycling coordinators who come up with creative uses for waste may find opportunities in other fields as well. For example, recycling of computers and computer parts is a growing area. Some with knowledge in this area have founded their own companies or work for computer manufacturers.

REQUIREMENTS

High School

Recycling coordinators need a variety of skills, so taking a variety of classes in high school is a good start. Classes in business, economics, and civics are a good idea to help build an understanding of the public sector in which most recycling coordinators work. Knowledge of how local governments and markets for recycled materials function is something you will need to know later, and civics and economics courses provide this framework. English and speech classes are vital to developing good oral and written communication skills that you use to spread the word about the importance of recycling. Mathematics and science will prove useful in setting recycling goals and understanding how recycling helps the environment.

Postsecondary Training

Until recently, people with all different types of backgrounds and experience were becoming recycling coordinators. Enthusiasm, an understanding of recycling issues, and business acumen were more important than any specific degree or professional background. This is still true to some extent, as colleges generally don't offer degrees in recycling coordination. Instead, a bachelor's degree in environmental studies or a related area and strong communication skills are desirable. Some schools offer minors in integrated waste management. Classes may include public policy, source reduction, transformation technology (composting/waste energy) and landfills, according to the Environmental Careers Organization (ECO).

Other Requirements

Useful personal skills include good communication and people skills for interacting with staff, contractors, government officials, and the public. Leadership, persuasiveness, and creativity (the ability to think of new ways to use collected materials, for example) also are important.

EXPLORING

You can start to explore a career as a recycling coordinator by getting familiar with the issues involved in the field. Why is sorting garbage so costly? Why are some materials recycled and not others? Where are the markets? What are some creative uses for recyclable materials? Find out what's going on both nationally and in your area. Some states have more extensive recycling programs than others; for example, some have bottle deposit laws or other innovative programs to boost recycling efforts. Get to know who's doing what and what remains to be done. Read industry-related magazines; two informative publications are *Recycling Today* (http://www.recyclingtoday.com) and *Resource Recycling* (http://www.resource-recycling.com). A useful book that focuses on environmental career possibilities is *The Complete Guide to Environmental Careers in the 21st Century*, by the ECO.

Arrange a tour of a local material recovery facility and talk with the staff there. You might even volunteer to work for a recycling organization. Large and small communities often have groups that support recycling with fund drives and information campaigns. Also, most municipal public meetings and workshops are good places to learn about how you can help with recycling in your community.

EMPLOYERS

Recycling coordinators are almost exclusively employed by some level of government; they oversee recycling programs at the city, county, or state level. A limited number of recycling coordinators may find work with waste haulers that offer recycling coordination as part of their contracts to municipalities. Recycling coordinators work in communities of all sizes—from rural countywide programs to urban ones. When states first mandated recycling, larger counties that generated more waste generally were the first to hire recycling coordinators. However, as more states set and achieve higher recycling goals, smaller cities and even rural areas need someone to coordinate their growing programs. At the state level, state environmental protection agencies or community development agencies may employ coordinators to administer state grants to and advise local recycling programs all over the state. Large organizations, such as colleges or military bases, are other employers of recycling coordinators.

STARTING OUT

A first job as a recycling coordinator is most likely to be with a smaller municipal program. Most colleges have a network of career referral services for their graduates, and city or county governments with openings for recycling coordinators often use these services to advertise positions to qualified graduates. Positions at the state level also may be available. Someone with previous experience with waste management projects, issues, and operations, in addition to the right educational background, is likely to get the more sought-after positions in larger cities and state governments. You can get hands-on experience through internships, volunteering, cooperative education, summer employment, or research projects, says the ECO.

You can gain experience during summers off from college, or if necessary, after college by volunteering or serving an internship with a recycling program in your area. If internships aren't available, paid work at a waste facility is a way to earn money over the summer and learn the very basics of recycling. Volunteering for a waste management consulting firm or nonprofit environmental organization is another way to get practical experience with recyclables. Most colleges have their own recycling programs, and you may find part-time work during the school year in your own college's recycling program. Contact the physical plant operations department or student employment services at your school.

ADVANCEMENT

In most cases, the position of recycling coordinator is the top spot in the recycling program. Advancement isn't really an option, unless the coordinator moves to another, perhaps larger, municipal program, to a private employer, or in some cases, to a different field. There is a fair amount of turnover in the field because recycling coordinator positions, in many cases, are training ground for college graduates who eventually move on to other fields where they use skills they developed as recycling coordinators. Because recycling coordinators develop so many useful skills, they often find work in related fields, such as small business administration and nonprofit organizations or as government administrators.

Since many states have waste-handling projects, someone with good experience at the local level might move into a state-level job, such as *recycling expert,* a position in some states' waste-handling departments. Opportunities with private businesses that have in-house recycling needs or with solid waste management consultants or businesses might also constitute advancement. Finally, recycling coordinators also have the opportunity to expand their own programs. Through their efforts, a modest program with a limited staff and budget could blossom into a full-scale, profitable venture for the community. The coordinator could conceivably extend the scope of the program; improve links with state or local government officials, the public, and private business and industry; receive more funding; add staff; and otherwise increase the extent and prominence of the program.

EARNINGS

Salaries vary widely for recycling coordinators. Starting salaries range from $22,000 per year in smaller counties or cities to $40,000 and higher for coordinators in larger municipalities, according to *The Complete Guide to Environmental Careers in the 21st Century*. A salary survey conducted by the National Association of Counties puts the average starting wage in counties with populations under 25,000 at $19,568. The average starting wage in counties with populations of 100,000 to 249,999 was $41,968. Some of the highest salaries reported were in counties with populations over 1 million, such as Maricopa County, Arizona, where the starting wage was $60,507. Salaries vary in different regions of the country. Positions in areas with a higher cost of living, such as California, Arizona, New York, and Washington, D.C., for example, tend to pay more.

According to the U.S. Department of Labor, median annual earnings of environmental engineers were $57,780 in 2000. Those who worked for state governments had median annual earnings of $53,210. Environmental engineering technicians had median annual earnings of $34,000 in 2000. A 2001 salary survey by the National Association of Colleges and Employers reports that bachelor's degree candidates in environmental engineering received starting offers averaging $51,167 a year.

Benefits vary, but most local governments offer full-time employees a benefit package that generally includes paid health insurance; a retirement plan; and holiday, vacation, and sick pay.

WORK ENVIRONMENT

Recycling coordinators are essentially administrators. As such, they primarily work indoors, either in their offices or in meetings or giving speeches. Recycling coordinators need to watch costs, understand markets, and work within budgets. They should be able to be firm with contractors when necessary. They need to demonstrate good judgment and leadership, and they may need to justify their decisions and actions to city council members or others. Stresses are part of the job, including dealing with government bureaucracy, dips in community participation, services that fall short of expectations, fluctuating markets for recyclables, and other less-than-ideal situations.

Generally, recycling coordinators work 40 hours per week if they are full-time employees. Some positions may be part time, but for both work arrangements, working hours are generally during the day with weekends off. Occasionally, recycling coordinators may need to attend meetings in the evening, such as a county or city board meeting, or speak before a community group that meets at night. Sometimes facility or landfill tours that a recycling coordinator may arrange or participate in to generate publicity for the program may be offered on weekends. Also occasionally, recycling coordinators may leave the office setting to visit the material recovery facility, which can be noisy and dirty if compacting equipment and conveyers are running.

OUTLOOK

The outlook for municipal recycling coordinators is good. According to the National Recycling Coalition, the recycling and reuse industry consists of approximately 56,000 establishments that employ over 1.1 million people, generate an annual payroll of nearly $37 billion, and gross over $236 billion in annual revenues. As states strive to meet their increasingly ambitious waste-reduction and recycling goals, people who can make it happen on the local level are going to be crucial. Although the recycling industry is subject to business fluctuations, demand and new technologies have created a viable market for recycled materials.

The recycling industry is also subject to political and social trends. Jobs will decline under administrations that do not allocate as much money for environmental concerns. On the other hand, more jobs may become available as engineers and technicians are attracted by the higher salaries offered in more popular technology- and finance-oriented fields.

Nationwide, the waste management and recycling industries will be needing more people to run recovery facilities, design new recycling technologies, come up with new ways to use recyclables, and do related work. Private businesses are also expected to hire recycling coordinators to manage in-house programs.

FOR MORE INFORMATION

For up-to-date information on recycling, contact
American Forest and Paper Association
1111 19th Street, NW, Suite 800

Washington, DC 20036
Tel: 800-878-8878
Email: info@afandpa.org
http://www.afandpa.org

For environmental information, contact
Earthsystems.org
508 Dale Avenue
Charlottesville, VA 22903
Tel: 434-293-2022
Email: www@earthsystems.org
http://www.earthsystems.org

For information on education and training, contact
Environmental Careers Organization
179 South Street
Boston, MA 02111
Tel: 617-426-4375
http://www.eco.org

This organization provides technical information, education, training, outreach and advocacy services.
National Recycling Coalition
1325 G Street, NW, Suite 1025
Washington, DC 20005
Tel: 202-347-0450
Email: info@nrc-recycle.org
http://www.nrc-recycle.org

For information on solid waste management, contact
National Solid Wastes Management Association
4301 Connecticut Avenue, NW, Suite 300
Washington, DC 20008
Tel: 800-424-2869
http://www.nswma.org

INTERVIEW

David Robinson is the recycling coordinator/assistant managing director for the city of Philadelphia. He spoke with the editors of Careers in Focus: Environment *about his career and the recycling field in general.*

Q. Please describe the responsibilities of your job.

A. I do many things in my role as recycling coordinator. I manage day-to-day activities of an team of eight professionals. In addition to the day-to-day work, which includes obvious things like taking calls, attending hundreds of meetings, representing the city in city council and at the state house, I manage a $10 million budget, oversee 141 operations crew members, and design and purchase special recycling vehicles and equipment. I also prepare all public and internal reports regarding the state of the program and deliver many talks and presentations to colleagues and customers alike. I have a hand in just about anything else that is remotely recycling related.

Q. What is a typical work day like for you? Do your responsibilities and/or interactions vary greatly?

A. There is no typical day for me. I could be hosting foreign dignitaries, be in meetings all day, writing reports, or visiting a recycling facility. Each day is different.

Q. What is your work environment like? Does your job involve travel?

A. My work environment is typical government. There are many cubicles on a floor in the Municipal Services Building. My office, along with those of my senior staff, occupy a corner of the floor. The environment is fairly quiet and professional. Yes, I travel extensively. For example, I was invited to speak in Liverpool this year and my speaking calendar is generally jam-packed.

Q. What have you learned about the recycling field since you first started working in it?

A. I entered the field in 1985. Recycling was making a national comeback since its days in the early 1970s, when it was a cousin of the ecology movement. The realities of any business always differ from the hype. Typically, recyclables are mined from waste; therefore, the parent of this business is trash. One must learn about the waste business to understand the recycling business. Recycling, however, is so much more than cans, bottles, and papers. It involves social marketing and urban planning. There is a great deal of entrepreneurial spirit still in the business, but it involves unions and politics, and one must know markets and market trends. One must understand economics and budgeting. It also involves children and education and developing curricula for schools, vehicle and facility design and management, and of course, the bigger the program (or city), the more intense the politics involved.

**Q. What course of study did you pursue during and after col-
lege? Did this prepare you for your career?**

A. I studied journalism in college, which prepares you for anything.
I was a working journalist when I was recruited by the late
Mayor Harold Washington in Chicago to join his team as a city
planner. It was at that time that I was asked to figure out how to
use recycling as a job-creation tool for neighborhood-based
economic development. I haven't been completely away from the
business since then. I have taken courses and continue to stay on
top of the trends by visitation, conferences, and report sharing.

**Q. Did you complete any internships or special training for
this career?**

A. The industry was quite young when I started and there weren't
things like that offered. However, I have administered over 20 students internships over the years.

Q. What other types of positions have you held?

A. I was a journalist (a reporter for the *Detroit News* and an editor
at UPI and other news organizations), executive director for a
couple of community-based economic development organizations, partner of a successful public/government affairs agency,
deputy clerk of the Cook County Board, and assistant commis-
sioner for the Department of Streets and Sanitation in Chicago.
I have held many other odd in-between gigs.

**Q. How did you find your current job? What are the other
ways one could look for this type of position?**

A. The mayor's office recruited me. In order to find a position in
this field, you should attend conferences, read the trade magazines, and get to know key players in the industry.

**Q. What is the current outlook for growth and advancement
in your field?**

A. Recycling is going through shake out right now. Big players will
buy little ones and government programs are undergoing budg-
et-related changes. But the industry will survive. The areas that
I believe will see the greatest growth are e-cycling (electronics
recycling) and plastics recovery and disposition. Despite it being
a small percentage of the waste stream, there will be a growing
number of opportunities in e-cycling as more and more con-
sumers get new equipment and government puts restrictions on
the disposal of old equipment. Plastics have replaced glass as the

predominant packaging choice. Its high volume and low weight make it costly and time consuming to collect. Solve the plastics issue and your career in this business will be painted in gold.

Q. **What would you say are the most important skills and personal qualities for someone in your career?**

A. Being an excellent writer/communicator, having a strong strategic thinking capacity, patience, vision, broad knowledge (an excellent liberal arts education), and being curious and results driven.

Q. **What advice would you give to someone who is interested in pursuing a career in recycling?**

A. Get to know the business and the players. Once you get in this business, it is hard to get out because you can have several careers all wrapped up in a recycled bow.

Soil Scientists

OVERVIEW

Soil scientists study the physical, chemical, and biological characteristics of soils to determine the most productive and effective planting strategies. Their research aids in producing larger, healthier crops and more environmentally sound farming procedures.

HISTORY

Hundreds of years ago, farmers planted crops without restriction, unaware that soil could be depleted of necessary nutrients by overuse. When crops were poor, farmers often blamed the weather instead of their farming techniques. (Some parts of the world still blame supernatural forces for poor harvests.)

Soil, one of our most important natural resources, was taken for granted until its condition became too bad to ignore. An increasing population, moreover, made the United States aware that its own welfare depends on fertile soil capable of producing food for hundreds of millions of people.

Increasing concerns about feeding a growing nation brought agricultural practices into consideration and reevaluation. In 1862, the U.S. Department of Agriculture (USDA) was created to give farmers information about new crops and improved farming techniques. Although the department started small, today the USDA is one of the largest agencies of the federal government.

Following the creation of a separate federal agency, laws were created to further promote and protect farmers. The 1933 Agricultural Adjustment Act inaugurated a policy of giving direct government aid to farmers. Two years later, the Natural Resource Conservation Service developed after disastrous dust storms blew away millions of tons of valuable topsoil and destroyed fertile cropland throughout the midwestern states.

Since 1937, states have organized themselves into soil conservation districts. Each local division coordinates with the USDA, assigning soil scientists and *soil conservationists* to help local farmers establish and maintain farming practices that will use land in the wisest possible ways.

THE JOB

Soil is formed by the breaking of rocks and the decay of trees, plants, and animals. It may take as long as 500 years to make just one inch of topsoil. Unwise and wasteful farming methods can destroy that inch of soil in just a few short years. In addition, rainstorms may carry thousands of pounds of precious topsoil away and dissolve necessary chemicals to grow healthy crops through a process called erosion. Soil scientists work with engineers to address these issues.

Soil scientists spend much of their time outdoors, tramping over fields, advising farmers on crop rotation or fertilizers, assessing the amount of field drainage, and taking soil samples. After researching an area, they may suggest certain crops to farmers to protect bare earth from the ravages of the wind and weather.

Soil scientists may also specialize in one particular aspect of the work. For example, they may work as a *soil mapper* or *soil surveyor*. These specialists study soil structure, origin, and capabilities through field observations, laboratory examinations, and controlled experimentation. Their investigations are aimed at determining the most suitable uses for a particular soil.

Soil fertility experts develop practices that will increase or maintain crop size. They must consider both the type of soil and the crop planted in their analysis. Various soils react differently when exposed to fertilizers, soil additives, crop rotation, and other farming techniques.

All soil scientists work in the laboratory. They examine soil samples under the microscope to determine bacterial and plant-food components. They also write reports based on their field notes and analyses done within the lab.

Soil science is part of the science of agronomy, which encompasses crop science. Soil and crop scientists work together in agricultural experiment stations during all seasons, doing research on crop production, soil fertility, and various kinds of soil management.

Some soil and crop scientists travel to remote sections of the world in search of plants and grasses that may thrive in this country and contribute to our food supply, pasture land, or soil replenishing efforts. Some scientists go overseas to advise farmers in other countries on how to treat their soils. Those with advanced degrees teach college agriculture courses and conduct research projects.

REQUIREMENTS

High School
If you're interested in pursuing a career in agronomy, you should take college preparatory courses covering subjects such as math, science, English, and public speaking. Science courses, such as Earth science, biology, and chemistry, are particularly important to take. Since much of your future work will involve calculations, you should take four years of high school math. You can learn a lot about farming methods and conditions by taking agriculture classes if your high school offers them. Computer science courses are also a good opportunity to become familiar with this technology. You should also take English and speech courses. Soil scientists must write reports and orally present their findings, and you will need excellent communication skills.

Postsecondary Training
A bachelor's degree in agriculture or soil science is the minimum educational requirement to become a soil scientist. Typical courses include physics, geology, bacteriology, botany, chemistry, soil and plant morphology, soil fertility, soil classification, and soil genesis.

Research and teaching positions usually require higher levels of education. Most colleges of agriculture also offer master's and doctoral degrees. In addition to studying agriculture or soil science, students can specialize in biology, chemistry, physics, or engineering.

Certification or Licensing
Though not required, many soil scientists may seek certification to enhance their careers. The American Society of Agronomy offers certification programs in the following areas: crop advisory, agronomy, crop science, soil science, plant pathology, and weed science. In order

to be accepted into a program, applicants must meet certain levels of education and experience.

Other Requirements

Soil scientists must be able to work effectively both on their own and with others on projects, either outdoors or in the lab. Technology is used increasingly in this profession; an understanding of word processing, the Internet, multimedia software, databases, and even computer programming can be useful in the profession. Soil scientists spend many hours outdoors in all kinds of weather, so they must be able to endure sometimes difficult and uncomfortable physical conditions. They must be detail-oriented to do accurate research, and they should enjoy solving puzzles—figuring out, for example, why a crop isn't flourishing and what fertilizers should be used.

EXPLORING

The National FFA Organization can introduce you to the concerns of farmers and researchers. A 4-H club can also give you valuable experience in agriculture. Contact the local branch of these organizations, your county's soil conservation department, or other government agencies to learn about regional projects. If you live in an agricultural community, you may be able to find opportunities for part-time or summer work on a farm or ranch.

EMPLOYERS

Most soil scientists work for state or federal departments of agriculture. However, they may also work for less obvious public employers, such as land appraisal boards, land-grant colleges and universities, and conservation departments. Soil scientists who work overseas may be employed by the U.S. Agency for International Development.

Soil scientists are needed in private industries as well, such as agricultural service companies, banks, insurance and real estate firms, food products companies, wholesale distributors, and environmental and engineering consulting groups. Private firms may hire soil scientists for sales or research positions.

STARTING OUT

In the public sector, college graduates can apply directly to the Resources Conservation Service of the Department of Agriculture, the Department of the Interior, the Environmental Protection Agency, or

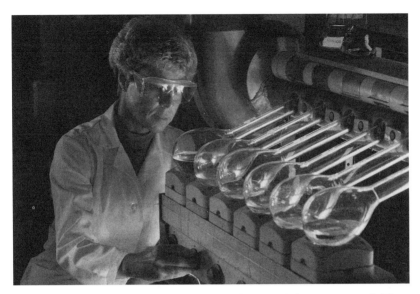

Soil scientists divide their time between field and laboratory work. This scientist is conducting a test on soil fertility. *(Corbis)*

other state government agencies for beginning positions. University placement services generally have listings for these openings as well as opportunities available in private industry.

ADVANCEMENT

Salary increases are the most common form of advancement for soil scientists. The nature of the job may not change appreciably even after many years of service. Higher administrative and supervisory positions are few in comparison with the number of jobs that must be done in the field.

Opportunities for advancement will be higher for those with advanced degrees. For soil scientists engaged in teaching, advancement may translate into a higher academic rank with more responsibility. In private business firms, soil scientists have opportunities to advance into positions such as department head or research director. Supervisory and manager positions are also available in state agencies such as road or conservation departments.

EARNINGS

According to the U.S. Department of Labor, median earnings in 2000 for agricultural scientists were $52,160. The lowest 10 percent earned less than $31,910; the middle 50 percent earned between $40,720 and $66,370; and the highest 10 percent, $83,740.

Federal salaries for soil scientists were higher; in 2001, they made an average of $58,878 a year. Government earnings greatly depend on levels of experience and education. Those with doctorates and a great deal of experience may be qualified for higher government positions, with salaries ranging from $70,000 to $90,000. Other than short-term research projects, most jobs offer health and retirement benefits in addition to your annual salary.

WORK ENVIRONMENT

Most soil scientists work 40 hours a week. Their job is varied, ranging from fieldwork collecting samples, to labwork analyzing their findings. Some jobs may involve travel, even to foreign countries. Other positions may include teaching or supervisory responsibilities for field training programs.

OUTLOOK

The *Occupational Outlook Handbook* reports that employment within the field of soil science is expected to grow more slowly than the average through 2010. The career of soil scientist is affected by the government's involvement in farming studies; as a result, federal and state budget cuts will limit funding for this type of job. However, private businesses will continue to demand soil scientists for research and sales positions. Companies dealing with seed, fertilizers, or farm equipment are examples of private industries that hire soil scientists.

Technological advances in equipment and methods of conservation will allow scientists to better protect the environment, as well as improve farm production. Scientists' ability to evaluate soils and plants will improve with more precise research methods. Combine-mounted yield monitors will produce data as the farmer crosses the field, and satellites will provide more detailed field information. With computer images, scientists will also be able to examine plant roots more carefully.

A continued challenge facing future soil scientists will be convincing farmers to change their current methods of tilling and chemical treatment in favor of environmentally safer methods. They must encourage farmers to balance increased agricultural output with the protection of our limited natural resources.

FOR MORE INFORMATION

ASA offers Exploring Careers in Agronomy, Crops, Soils, and Environmental Sciences, *and also has information on certification and college chapters. For details, contact*
American Society of Agronomy (ASA)
677 South Segoe Road
Madison, WI 53711
Tel: 608-273-8080
http://www.agronomy.org

For information on seminars, issues affecting soil scientists, and educational institutions offering soil science programs, contact
National Society of Consulting Soil Scientists
PMB 700, 325 Pennsylvania Avenue, SE
Washington, DC 20003
Tel: 800-535-7148
http://www.nscss.org

For the career brochure Soils Sustain Life, *contact*
Soil Science Society of America
677 South Segoe Road
Madison, WI 53711
Tel: 608-273-8095
http://www.soils.org

Index

Entries and page numbers in **bold** indicate major treatment of a topic.